SMART
PRACTICE
Rocket Fuel For Your Skills
*A Systematic Approach To Get Better
At Anything*

Jeff Scheetz

Published by BAM-ZOOM!
Kansas City, MO U.S.

ISBN 978-1-7320110-0-7

For a FREE bonus ebook, and to stay connected with ongoing tips and updates, go to:

www.smartpracticeacademy.com

For all my family (both 2 legged and 4 legged) who are why I strive to be better today than I was yesterday. To my Mom who taught me to appreciate poetry and memorize wisdom quotes from as early of an age as I can remember.

… For my Dad, because he always had time to take me fishin'.

CONTENTS

Introduction

She looked focused. With one fluid motion she took two steps backwards, spun to the right in a 180 degree turn and then backed up rapidly launching directly into a backflip. Without missing a beat she took one step forward and leaped off my back 8 feet in the air and caught the frisbee between her teeth before falling gracefully back to earth without a hair out of place.

Killian is a world champion frisbee dog.

She was born on a farm in a litter of unwanted puppies. She was handed over to a local animal rescue, where I adopted her. She is a mix of Australian Shepherd, Border Collie and who knows what else.

But do you know what is really amazing? She is just like you and me. She wasn't born with those awesome skills, she had to develop them. Through systematic practice of the right things in the right way, Killian went from unwanted farm pup to world champ.

Do you have a skill that you would like to develop? Something you'd like to get better at? Most of us can think of several things we would like to improve in our lives. And yet, we often find ourselves stuck in the proverbial rut, not knowing the right steps to take to get better. Or even worse, sometimes we try something, and when it doesn't work we get frustrated and give up.

In this book I'll show you the complete system I've developed for getting better at anything. I call it SMART Practice. I break down every component that contributes to getting better. Step by step I'll help you determine the most important things to work on so you don't waste time. I'll show you how to assess your current skills and schedule your time in a unique and effective way. You'll learn how to organize your thinking so you can get the biggest bang for your practice buck. We'll also examine new scientific research and implement new techniques to keep practice fun and interesting!

My journey to develop the SMART practice system was born out of that same frustration we have all felt. I had lots of things I wanted to get better at, but had no real organized method to help me. I was up against the same immovable obstacle we all face; that there are only 24 hours in a day. That doesn't seem to be enough time to tackle everything we want. My inefficient methods of working on stuff just led to lots of wheel spinning and very little progress.

I knew the only way for me to get better was to get more effective and more efficient with the time I had to practice. So I started to organize, study, research, and track how to get the most out of my practice time. I did this across a wide variety of skills I was working on. Everything from playing guitar, Tae Kwon Do, learning chess, target shooting, even racing dirt bikes. I had crazy stacks of notebooks everywhere detailing all manner of practice methods I had tried and documented what worked and what didn't.

Once I felt like I had discovered some things that were making a big difference in my progress, I wanted to see if these methods would work for others.

Over the years I tested my methods on thousands of music

students and tracked all the results. I started to see patterns. There were some things that worked for some students, but not for others. However, there were some things that seemed to work for everyone! These were more "universal" practice truths that just helped everyone. So I started testing it on other people I helped coach in other skills. I found these universal principles of practice worked whether a student was trying to get better at golf, playing piano, throwing a frisbee, dog training or even casting a fly rod.

These concepts make up the SMART practice core system and are the foundation for getting better at anything. That is the good news, once you learn the principles and how the system works, then you can apply it to various skills in your life where you want to see improvement.

I'm really excited to share this system with you and see where it can take you. It took Killian from unwanted farm pup to world champ, and without a doubt it can help you get better at anything as well.

Part One: Perspective

1: What Practice Is and Isn't

Practice. Just the mention of the word conjures up powerful feelings. We have been aware from an early age that people who have achieved greatness have gotten there by practicing. We have been told "Practice makes perfect". We have heard the story of the young musician who is walking in New York City and asks a gentleman "How do I get to Carnegie Hall?" The gentleman simply replies, "Practice." We have most likely experienced practicing first hand; "You guys go out in left field and practice catching some balls", "Go to your room and practice your clarinet", "The band is coming over tonight for practice running through the setlist", "I'm giving a speech this weekend and I need to practice it", "I need to practice for my drivers Ed exam","I need to go to the range and practice my drives", and so on.

However, although we know practice is important, and have been taught it is the number one ingredient in excelling at any skill, why is it so many of us still struggle to improve on things we want to be better at?

I believe it is not that we don't know we *need* to practice, it's that most of us have never really mastered *how* to practice.

For some of us, perhaps our very perception of practice has blocked us from seeing the need to get better at it. What do you think of when you hear the word "practice?"

In a recent poll, when given the word "practice" and asked to write down the thing they most associated with that word, the overwhelming majority of people wrote one of two things; sports, or music.

I see that perception of practice repeated over and over, sports and music are things you *practice*. It makes sense because practice is indeed necessary to achieve proficiency in both of those skill sets. But what if you want to get better at other things? What do you do then? What if you want to become a better writer? Or get better at speaking Spanish? Or become a better parent, football coach, or just get better at being productive?

Could you just get better at those things by being really hopeful? Maybe thinking positively about how awesome you are will magically make you better at them? Or just doing them occasionally will move you to the front of the pack?

I believe that in each of these cases, the most efficient and effective way to get better, is with practice. More precisely, using the right kind of complete practice plan that is specifically designed to help you improve in a systematic way.

While we are talking about perceptions, the other problem that can interfere with our improvement is this idea that we *have* to practice, instead of we *want* to practice, or we *get* to practice. You should think of practice as something that you are lucky you get to do and be excited for the opportunity to get better!

Sometimes negative connotations can also stem from environmental pressures; "If you don't practice your violin you're not getting any supper." Yikes! It's no wonder we can develop an aversion to practicing! Or just daily drudgery like "Well, I have to take the kids to soccer practice," can instill an image of how you perceive practice. If you really think about it, for most of us, "practice" has not been framed in our minds in a positive way.

Therefore, the number one thing we have to get clear about at the outset is our perception or understanding of what practice is and how we relate to it. Practice is the fuel that makes the engine of improvement run. Whether you are learning a new skill or trying to improve an existing one, following an organized practice system will help you get maximum results from the time you put in. Practicing the right things in the right way is the best and most efficient way to get better at anything.

It also helps to not only look at what practice is, but what it isn't. In my years of teaching music I can think of many students who struggled to improve, even though they said they were putting in the hours on their instrument. When I would ask them if they practiced that week they would say "Heck yeah! Last night I played for 3 hours." But when asked to define exactly what they did for those hours, their response was often something like, "I had a couple of friends come over and we jammed on Black Sabbath, played some video games and ordered pizza!" While that could technically be considered "putting in some hours"… it's not really practicing.

K. Anders Ericsson is one of the leading researchers in the field of expertise. He has studied what it takes to achieve a high level of skill in numerous disciplines. His research shows that proper practice, what he calls "Deliberate" practice, "Requires effort and is not inherently enjoyable" and that, "Individuals are motivated to practice because practice improves performance".[1] So it is not just about fun or the short term enjoyment, but rather the joy that will come from what it will eventually give you.

This can be a difficult concept, especially for very creative persons or for those of us who can be impatient. Often our DNA says "Let's Go! Let's jam on this now!" We don't want to take the time to prepare or get too organized, we just want to get right to it. However, if you really want to improve, you have to change from a mindset of just messing around when you practice, to one of actually following a practice system that helps you work on the things you need to do in order to get better. You need to get a plan. As coach John Wooden said; "Failing to prepare is preparing to fail."

So practice IS what you need to get better, but it has to be the right kind of practice to really be effective. In the next chapters of this book I will be distilling the various elements of what makes effective practice. I have built up the techniques and methods of practicing you'll find here over many years of study and trial and error. Once I learned the impact of practicing this way, and started teaching it to students and seeing their results, there was no going back.

2: Behind the Curtain

The first time I really realized how powerful it could be to practice something the right way, I was about 13 years old.

I grew up on a farm in rural Iowa, where it was fairly normal for local farm boys to learn how to shoot a shotgun at an early age. So at the age of 13, I remember having three friends come over to my house where we all took our guns out behind the barn to shoot "clay pigeons". Some with more sophistication may call that shooting "sporting clays" or shooting "skeet". But to a bunch of sun tanned shirtless boys firing over a cornfield in rural Iowa on a warm summer day, they were just clay pigeons.

They basically looked like little clay UFOs that would fly across the sky until they either exploded with a direct hit from the shotgun, or floated to the ground in the field where we would go pick them up to reuse.

We had just bought a contraption that had a spring loaded arm that you had to cock back and place a clay pigeon in there, and then pull a string to hurl it into the air. This was a decidedly upgraded method from our previous device which was really just a glorified baseball bat with a shelf to hold the targets you then had to launch into the air by hand.

I was a decent shot already, as was Jack, one of the other

boys. The other two were not very good and after a few misses they got bored and laid their guns down to pursue more achievable results by throwing rocks through the already broken out window of the barn. Jack and I continued to shoot and found that we were pretty close to hitting the same percentage of targets. The day came to a close, but in typical competitive teenage boys fashion, we said we would get back together in a few weeks and finish the competition to see who was "the best." (That is important to teenage boys you know.)

When I thought about the looming rematch, I decided I needed to get better if I was going to out shoot Jack. This was of course at a time before there were videos to watch on YouTube or Google to learn the finer points of the art of target shooting. So with no instruction, I went out with my shotgun to practice. But then something happened. It suddenly seemed to make innate sense to me that in order to improve, I should look at all the little parts or components that went into my shooting form. Rather than just go out and shoot, I first focused on those parts.

I decided that before the trigger was even pulled, I had to get the gun up to my shoulder. (Our loose rules had said we had to start with the gun by our side before the target was thrown.) So I just started slowly putting the gun up to my shoulder, pulling the stock against my cheek, feeling the balance. Over and over again I went through this motion making little changes each time until it seemed right. I gradually started to line my eye up with the sight and feel my finger on the trigger. But I never actually shot. I was convinced that getting this motion as fast and fluid as I could would help me gain more time to then follow the target and shoot.

Not a shot was fired at my house for the first two weeks. Yet everyday I went out and practiced for hours and hours.

Once I started actually shooting, it seemed effortless.

It was a little over a month before we were able to get together again. Only Jack and one of the other boys came out. Jack claimed he hadn't practiced much, but since we lived on the same country road only a half a mile apart, I knew that wasn't entirely true because I had been hearing shotgun blasts coming from the general direction of his house for the last several weeks. The other boy said he didn't practice and that was evident from the first shot, which was a miss. However, I told them I had practiced but not just shooting, I worked on my stance, raising the gun into position, going through the motion of following an imaginary moving target, and yes, for the last few days I had actually been shooting. They basically looked at me like I was nuts… until I started shooting.

Not only did I out shoot Jack that day. It wasn't even close. It was like I was in a whole different league than he was. The shots that before had been a little sloppy for me or the uncomfortable "lucky" hits, were now machine like in their precision. I had literally gone from just being a decent shot a month before to now hitting almost all the targets. I had turbo charged my ability. Jack was frustrated and bewildered, and after a few rounds where he hit less than half as many targets as I did, decided to stop shooting and suggested we do something else. We never shot together again.

That moment for me when I saw the power of proper practice, of what I later developed more thoroughly and came to call SMART Practice, changed the way I have approached everything since then. It's like once you actually SEE something happen, then you're a true believer. I had seen the inner workings, figured it out, cracked the code, in spite of the admonition from the Wizard, I had indeed paid attention to the man behind the curtain.

3: The Surge

Over the past 10 years or so there's been a real surge of interest in peak performance and what has come to be called the science of expertise. There have been many new books written on the subject, and many new studies done. This has been really exciting for me. For my entire life I have been interested in, studied, and endeavored to understand the various ways that humans can enhance their abilities.

Of course throughout history there has been interest in human potential. We have come up with all sorts of methods to improve. Everything from following common sense directives like, "Eat less and exercise more" for better health, to wearing "tin foil hats" type of headgear to keep others from reading our minds and draining our energy! While the effectiveness (and craziness) of the methods and ideas from the past varies greatly, there are certainly some things that over time have become *principles* due to their staying power and success.

Yet many of the methods from the past that were once just "the way you do it" have been challenged by new findings that open the door to a possible better way. Sorting out what works and what doesn't in the midst of all the opinions and options can be a daunting task. One of the most talked about subjects in conversations on talent and getting better is the Nature vs. Nurture debate.

This debate has raged on throughout the ages. If you fall on the nature side, you think that talent is innate and you either have it or you don't. If you are a nurture evangelist, you believe that talent is developed. The actual term "nature versus nurture" was originally coined in 1869 by Francis Galton, who was a cousin to Charles Darwin. (Galton was entrenched on the nature side.) However, the concept of where a person's talent or ability comes from has been debated since the days of the ancient Greeks, so it could certainly be considered an ongoing discussion!

One of the books that has helped drive the surge of new enthusiasm for studying performance is Malcolm Gladwell's *Outliers: The Story of Success*. He tackled the nature vs nurture question from an investigative journalist angle. For example he helped uncover the reason the overwhelming majority of professional hockey players in Canada had birthdays in the months of January, February, and March. Gladwell tells us it starts early in a hockey players development, in the junior leagues. "It's simply that in Canada the eligibility cutoff for age class hockey is January 1. A boy who turns 10 on January 2, then, could be playing alongside someone who doesn't turn ten until the end of the year, and at that age, in preadolescence, a twelve month gap in age represents an enormous difference in physical maturity."[1]

That age difference would look like "potential" to coaches who would then spend more time with those boys, and allow them to play more games. It would lead to them being selected for all star teams where they would get to play with the best of the best. In most practices and drills they would basically look like the cream of the crop compared to the other boys who were a little less developed. Of course this likely has a profound effect on the player's self confidence and enthusiasm for the game as well. (You tend to commit to something you think you're good at, especially if others reinforce that by telling you how good you are and how much potential you have.)

Many of Gladwell's examples showed that environmental and circumstantial situations could be the tipping point that pushed someone into what would be considered a "more talented" zone. The interesting thing that sometimes gets lost in books about peak performance, is that on the nurture side, it isn't just about conditioning, practicing, or consciously doing something. Other factors contribute such as, where you live, when were you born, decisions you make that may not be directly tied to your particular skill but have brought you to where you are.

It can be said that luck could certainly play a roll as well. Luck is a hard thing to measure. Because while there does seem to be "right place, right time, look what happened" events that occur, luck can also cross over into the nurture category. Your genes are what they are, but the nurturing you do can put you in fortunate situations. What may look like luck to others is often just a cascading series of decisions and choices you have made throughout your life that makes you suddenly appear lucky. As Douglas MacArthur said "The best luck of all is the luck you make for yourself." There is no doubt that being in the right place at the right time can sometimes give the appearance of some unseen force at work.

4: Lucky or Good?

The smoke was so thick you could barely see the stage if you were more than 20 feet away. However, that didn't stop "Rory Storm and the Hurricanes" from launching into their set of rock and roll. The crowd was very appreciative, and quite raucous. The club was a popular watering hole in Hamburg, Germany. The year was 1961.

The band's drummer had spent time earlier in the evening during their break checking out another band across the street, because as he put it, "They were doing better stuff. They had a good style." Over the next few months he hung out with that band on many occasions as the two bands always seemed to be playing in the same cities. That other band was The Beatles, and the drummer playing with Rory was Ringo Starr.

Ringo says, "We'd all played the same venues and, at the time, Rory and the Hurricanes used to be top of the bill. One morning, I was in bed, a knock came at the door, and Beatles manager Brian Epstein said, 'Would you play a lunchtime session at the Cavern with the Beatles?' And I said, 'Okay, okay, I'll get out of bed,' and I went down and played. Their drummer wasn't well so they needed someone to fill in for the session, so I went and played, that's all there was to it." After 6 months of filling in occasionally Ringo says he got one more call. "Brian called and asked if I would join the Beatles. I said, 'Yeah, I'd love to'."[1]

Of course as they say, the rest is history. So was Ringo's success Nature, Nurture, or just dumb luck?

This is a good example of how it isn't always as cut and dried as just looking at one simple predictor of success. The nature side of what genes Ringo was born with probably wasn't the reason for his success. His path to being one of the most well known drummers in history had more to do with nurture, but maybe not the exact nurture that many of us think about.

Especially in the world of self improvement, the "nurture" that most subscribe to is more of the direct "You practice for X hours and you see X results." While that is certainly nurturing, it is only a small part of what it means to be shaped into who you are instead of born into who you are. It is usually a longer path. In Ringo's case his nurturing wasn't just "Practice X hours, get X results," it was more like "Get interested in music, decide to play the drums, borrow money from Grandfather to buy drums, start playing with local groups, practice x hours, play with more bands, become friends with other bands, drink copious amounts of alcohol at other bands gigs and hang out until daylight, practice more, play some more gigs, then become successful." That is a lot of nurturing! Oh, and make sure you get out of bed to answer the door when someone's knocking!

A common thread you'll find in many of the new books and studies on peak performance and the science of expertise is the prevailing thought that it's nurture over nature when it comes to creating excellence. In other words, experts aren't born, they're made. By analyzing and studying expert's methods, and then following in their footsteps, we too can become world class at anything.

Having worked with thousands of individual students over the years, I have certainly accumulated enough experiential data to develop my own theory on this. There is no question in my mind that practicing the right things in the right way and nurturing your development works every time to move you forward. However, I also tend to agree with the view that says it's not always just an either/or answer, but the better answer lies in some combination of what you are born with and what you develop that gives you the ultimate level to which you can reach.

David Epstein in *The sports Gene: Inside the Science of Extraordinary Athletic Performance* says, "The broad truth is that nature and nurture are so interlaced in any realm of athletic performance that the answer is always: it's both."[2]

The great news for all of us who aspire to get better at something is that whether you believe in nature, nurture, or some combination, it is universally agreed that whatever your skill level currently is, you can take steps to improve it!

That is what this book is about. How to get better. Was Tiger Woods born with a special "golf gene", or did his hours of practicing at 3 years old make him a legend? When all is said and done, for us right now... it doesn't matter! What matters is there is no doubt that whoever you are, wherever you are, if you want to get better at something, you CAN! So celebrate! Give a hardy Yeeeehaaaw! Sometimes the debate on where talent comes from gets too much attention and distracts us from the simple fact that has been proven over and over again: practicing the right things in the right way will make you better!

5: **10,000 Hours**

Perhaps the contribution that Malcom Gladwell is most widely known for in regards to the discussion on becoming an expert is the "10,000 hour rule." This is the theory that says it takes 10,000 hours to master a skill. This "rule" has stirred up some controversy and fiery opinions as to how accurate it really is, but it has definitely become part of the lexicon of the science of expertise. Can we put an exact number on the hours required? I would say it greatly depends on how those hours are actually spent!

The general idea about the 10,000 hour rule was coined by Gladwell, and he based it on the research done by K. Anders Ericsson where Ericsson and his colleagues studied violin students and their hours of practice. But did Ericsson actually give that exact number of hours? In a paper written by Ericsson in 2012 he said:

"In fact, the 10,000 hour rule was invented by Malcolm Gladwell who cited our research on expert musicians as a stimulus for his provocative generalization to a magical number. Our research found that the best violinists reported having spent a remarkably large number of hours engaged in solitary practice, when in fact, 10,000 hours was the average of the best group, and most of the best musicians had accumulated substantially fewer hours of practice at age 20."[1]

So while the 10,000 hour rule may leave a few questions hanging, to me it doesn't matter. Why? Because once again, we know that practicing the right things in the right way will make you better! How much better will depend on a few things, including how many hours you put in. If you want to put in 10,000 you will most likely get really good, but if you just put in 247 hours you will be better than you are right now! That is the point that is lost in all this debate on expertise and how many thousands of hours it takes to become the best in the world. *Most folks just want to get better!*

Through many years of working with guitar students, I would see time and again someone come to me who had been playing for 10 plus years and still hadn't achieved much proficiency. These were hobbyists that had been playing just for fun but were frustrated because they hadn't improved very much. This led me to tell them that "It's not the years you've been playing, it's the hours." This however didn't really do it justice as I also saw students who put in many hours on the wrong things or practicing in the wrong way and not see the results they wanted either.

My formula eventually became; *It's not the years, it's not the hours, it's what you are actually doing during those hours and how you are doing it that will determine your success!*

Part Two: Science Merges With Art

6: The Merge

I often say that SMART Practice is where the Science of practice Merges with the ART of practice. While that's certainly a catchy slogan, it's also an important concept for anyone looking to get better at anything. Science and art may seen like an unlikely combination, but together they can be deadly when it comes to self improvement.

SMART Practice

Where the **S**cience of Practice
Merges with the
ART of **Practice**

The influx of new scientific data on how our brains react to various situations, decisions and movements has been a huge leap forward in understanding why some methods of improvement seem to get better results than others. As one example, we can now use neuroimaging to allow us to detect more clearly what stimuli causes dopamine to be released. Dopamine is a chemical that has many functions in the brain. The release of dopamine is associated with pleasure, attention, motivation, memory, and can help drive us to rewards. It's this neurotransmitter that has been a hot topic in the world of expertise for some time due to the effects it has on multiple areas that are of interest to those looking for peak performance.

But what if you are standing at the driving range, it's late at night, you're tired, your body is sore from getting up early to take the kids to school and working all day. What the heck does some fancy study about dopamine have to do with this bucket of balls you are about to hit?

Good question.

I tell my students the real benefit of looking at the science behind practicing is in helping you setup your practice time to take advantage of everything you can. From dopamine releases to focus points to memorization techniques that help you retain information acquired at practice. The nice thing about the scientific aspect of practice is it takes some of the uncertainty out of things and puts you at ease to just focus on doing the task at hand instead of wondering what is actually going to help. It is good to know that when you practice and do *this*, then *that* will happen. So You KNOW it will work because the data is there to back it up. It gives you an incredible boost of confidence knowing what you are doing will pay off, so you won't question whether or not you are just spinning your wheels.

When we look at what is happening in the brain during any activity we see a lot going on. A quick perusal of scientific studies on brain activity and function will show you what happens in your brain when you are writing, playing chess, meditating, doing motor learning, telling jokes, and yes, even playing jazz.

A John Hopkins research project led by Dr. Charles Limb, a surgeon and jazz musician, noted that, "Within jazz improvisation, certain emotional states may open musicians to deeper flow states or more robust stimulation of reward centers."[1] Groovy.

Many studies on brain activity use a functional magnetic resonance imaging (fMRI) machine. This is a brain scanning machine that illuminates areas of the brain responding to various stimuli, identifying which areas are active while a person is involved in some activity.

As the researchers studied these jazz musicians using the fMRI technology, they gained insight into the complexities of what happens in the brain while two musicians are trading solos. Musicians have been able to express in their own way how they feel when they jam with one another, but that is not always easy to convert into a language that normal people can understand. (Ever talk to "jazz cats?") So this study sheds some light on the data from a scientific standpoint, which can be used in other areas.

One of the interesting things that fMRI has shown us is how merely visualizing something you are about to practice can create similar brain activity as actually doing it. This of course backs up what we already know from practical experience; that just visualizing or seeing the skill being done perfectly in your mind's eye can help you improve. This science will assure you that you can feel confident in your visualization techniques!

Some science is quantifiable and easily repeatable. Some however, is believed to be true, but may not come with the easy step by step method to call it up at will. "Flow" is in that category.

The term "Flow" was coined by psychologist Mihaly Csikszentmihalyi. His groundbreaking book *Flow: The Psychology of Optimal Experience*, delved deep into how people reach optimum happiness, and how to get into that state. Csíkszentmihályi himself defines flow and says it is, "Being completely involved in an activity for its own sake. The ego falls away. Time flies. Every action, movement, and thought follows inevitably from the previous one, like playing jazz. Your whole being is involved, and you're using your skills to the utmost."[2]

In the world of sports or high level performance, this is sometimes known as being "in the zone." Like when Jordan scores 55 points against the Knicks and says the basket seemed like it was 10 feet wide. The game becomes effortless. That's in the zone.

Steven Kotler in the book *The Rise of Superman: Decoding the Science of Ultimate Human Performance,* talks about both internal and external Flow "Triggers." While flow is elusive, he outlines a series of ways to "get into flow." According to Kotler, "Just as flow states have external triggers, conditions in the outer environment that create more flow, they also have internal triggers, conditions in our inner environment that create more flow."[3]

Even if there are some semi predictable ways to increase your odds of being in flow, the question is: Will it help us practice? Flow is of course the holy grail at performance time. That is when being in flow really shines, takes the gold medal, rises against all odds. But there is discussion as to not only if it is possible to get into flow during practice, but if it is even desired!

When we are really doing the right things in practice, it is more intentional, analytical, and adjustable. Our thinking as we practice is usually more about making sure our technique is right and noticing anything we need to tweak. Flow is usually just the opposite: Let it go, let it happen. However, depending on what skill you are practicing flow may help take you to the place you need to become familiar with in order to perform at your best when it counts. In other words it may be helpful to get to know flow ahead of when you need it.

My general take on flow in practice is this; You can have an effective practice without dealing with flow at all. However, since I always encourage spending some of your practice time in *performance mode* it may make sense to practice triggering a flow state to test it out and push yourself to practice out there on the edge. The idea of practicing getting into flow then creates another paradigm. It is not flow during practice, it is practice to achieve flow. That makes sense. Add that to the list.

That's just a drop in the bucket of how we can view various science as it relates to practice. As we gain a deeper understanding of how to link up the myriad of scientific information with practical use, it gives us a much clearer explanation of what is happening as we practice. But I said SMART Practice is where the Science of practice Merges with the Art of practice. For the art side of the coin, that can be a little trickier because as is often the case with any kind of art, it's harder to put your finger on exactly what makes it work and what makes it good. If it was all just as simple as looking at scientific data and then everyone doing it the same way, that would be easy!

Part of the art is understanding that we are all unique beings with individual personalities and physical traits, living in very different constantly changing environmental conditions. So we have to come up with a practice system that can adapt to each person's needs while at the same time maintaining some connection to the scientific based methods that we know work.

As I developed the SMART Practice system, I kept this balance of science and art in mind. You start with things you know work, but build in flexibility for the individual.

I was tasked with helping a woman get better at throwing a frisbee. The good news was there was no way to go but up as she simply could not throw one at all. She would rear back and throw and it would go 5 yards and fly directly into the ground to the right!

Using the scientific data to come up with a practice plan in this instance was not enough. We had to get *artistic* with her plan, because her unique feature was hyper extended elbows. So when she extended her arm out in a normal backhand frisbee throwing motion, the joint of her elbow finished pointing straight up to the sky, instead of staying roughly perpendicular to the ground like most people. This caused her entire arm to roll over, repeatedly sending the disc to it's fateful crash into the ground.

In this case we had to ignore the normal steps of firing up a practice routine, and start with our focus on a completely separate goal of building a way to compensate for this difference. Once that was accomplished, then and only then were we able to get back to doing what the usual system or universal data would have us do. So the *art* of getting better in this case had to be called upon by way of finding a creative way to work around an obstacle. Then she could tackle the science of the organized practice system.

The good news is that it worked. Within 2 years she was winning world championships in distance throwing and setting world records. You have to look at what you are practicing, and then balance how much art and how much science it will take to accomplish what you want.

The purpose of this book isn't to delve deep into all the scientific variables that are out there. If you want to dig into that, there is research available on almost any element of practice. The SMART Practice System is about taking a look at some of the top level hands-on science, and putting it into practice in real world situations.

The great news is that we are constantly gaining more clarity on what we need to work on for any given skill. This will give us the snapshot we need to be able to mix in the art and scientific application to make our practice the most effective it can be!

7: Mindset

"All personal achievement starts in the mind of the individual."

W. Clement Stone

Long before Norman Vincent Peale wrote "The Power of Positive Thinking," or Napoleon Hill told us to "Think and Grow Rich," the idea that our minds had an important role in controlling our destiny was being put forth.

Even before Socrates said "To find yourself, think for yourself," Greek philosopher Heraclitus said, "Day by day, what you choose, what you think and what you do is who you become."

There is no question that there's enough evidence to prove that having a positive attitude can help bring about good things and having a negative one can take you in the other direction.

In more recent times the buzzwords of *Growth Mindset*, and *Fixed Mindset*, are sure to crop up in any discussion on learning or improving. In this dichotomy people with a Growth Mindset tend to believe they can get better, and consider where they currently are as just the starting point. They can develop their skills with effort. Folks with a Fixed Mindset think that there is a hard limit on what they are capable of, that basically they are born with a certain amount of intelligence and ability and that is just the way it is.

This of course is very similar to the Nature vs. Nurture debate we talk about elsewhere. Nature would certainly favor a Fixed Mindset while Nurture is all about Growth.

Stanford psychologist Carol Dweck has been on the cutting edge of these concepts for a number of years. She has done numerous studies with students and her book *Mindset: The New Psychology of Success* is often used as reference for anyone digging deeper into mindset. She discovered that students could be shaped into better students not only by the material they were learning, but also by how they viewed themselves to begin with. Professor Dweck says, "We found that students' mindsets—how they perceive their abilities—played a key role in their motivation and achievement, and we found that if we changed students' mindsets, we could boost their achievement. More precisely, students who believed their intelligence could be developed (a growth mindset) outperformed those who believed their intelligence was fixed (a fixed mindset)."[1]

Now, what does this have to do with SMART Practice? A lot.

If your Mindset is one of "This is just the way I am," then you probably don't think any amount of practice will make you better. Which means you will not have a lot of motivation to stick with a practice plan, or work through the rough spots.

However, with a Mindset that says "I can and will get better," you can't lose! Put that together with an organized practice plan and you are well on your way to improving!

Suffice it to say I am a believer in a Growth Mindset! The whole premise behind the SMART Practice system is that it is possible to get better at anything. Starting with the right positive mindset is important.

One thing about the Growth Mindset or the Nurture belief is that it is not *just* having a good mindset or positive thoughts that will make you better. You still have to do the work! But everything has to have a beginning and the beginning of getting better at something is your belief that you can.

Of course as we've seen, the idea that your success starts with what you believe is not new. As a matter of fact, before there were any fancy terms for it Henry Ford summed it up succinctly when he said; "Whether you believe you can, or believe you can't, you're right."

What is your mindset? Take some time to consider whether you really believe that practice can make you better, or if you secretly doubt that it will.

Tune up your mindset with these tips:

1. Acknowledge where you are. You may have a Growth Mindset in one area of your life, but a Fixed Mindset in another. "I am a really creative person and am really good at art, but I am terrible at math, and just don't get it." This would be a good example of looking at two areas of your life with different mindsets. So take a look at what you are doing right in the Growth areas and what is holding you back in the Fixed spots.

2. Look at things you have gotten better at and remember what your mindset was like. You most likely believed it was possible to get better, and took actions (like practicing) to get there. So tell yourself that can happen again!

3. Recognize that you have a choice. This is from Carol Dweck herself. "How you treat challenges, setbacks and criticism is up to you. You can interpret them with a fixed mindset as signs that your talents are lacking, or you can interpret them with a growth mindset as signs that you need to ramp up your strategies and effort, stretch yourself and expand your abilities. You decide."[2]

4. When I am in competitions, before I take the field I tell myself there are two outcomes possible. I am either going to *win*, or I am going to *learn*. That way even if I "lose" it helps me. Make yourself look at losing as learning and you will see your mindset and your skills move in the right direction!

5. Train yourself to apply *Lateral Thinking* to each task. Don't just settle for only one way to look at things, instead, ask yourself, "What are my options?" or "What can I do differently?" Edward De Bono who literally wrote the book on Lateral Thinking says, "No way of looking at things is too sacred to be reconsidered. No way of doing things is beyond improvement."[3]

Whether we call it a positive attitude, growth mindset, or what my Dad used to just refer to as "Right thinkin'," there is no doubt that your practice will benefit from this as a starting point!

8: Blocked or Random

He cleared the first jump by a foot, same with the next one. Now he dove into the tunnel at full speed and shot out the other side ready to scale the A-frame. But he stopped and looked around, and then headed over to another jump. He was off course.

So it usually is when training my dog Towser in agility. He had already went through this same layout of obstacles twice, and did it perfectly both times. In his mind I believe two thoughts are happening. One is, "I know I already did this perfectly, but if you are making me do it again I guess I better try something else." And the other is, "This is boring!"

Towser is a world champion Frisbee dog who just does agility for cross training, but he doesn't like to drill on something over and over. He loses interest if he thinks he has done it right and you want him to do it again.

The truth is we all get bored by repetitive tasks, and just that fact can make our practice less effective. Fortunately for us, research confirms that doing the same thing over and over may NOT always be the best way to practice!

(I for one love it when there is actually research that confirms what I want to do anyway!)

For most practice activities that require motion, we all

know that working on our motor learning or "muscle memory" is important. Getting movement down to the point where we don't have to consciously think about every aspect of it, but rather just do it is key to being able to focus on other things.

Blocked and Random Practice

There are a couple of schools of thought on practicing movements: *Blocked* practice and *Random* practice are two methods that have been discussed and debated by instructors and students for years.

Blocked practice is basically the method of doing the same thing over and over until you get it down, and then moving on to the next thing. Say you have 3 things you want to work on in a practice session. You would just drill on the first thing until you got it, or for a set number of minutes, and then do the same for the second and third things.

Random practice says you take those 3 things and mix them up. Do the first thing once, then the second a couple of times, then the third and so on.

Blocked practice is sometimes thought of as more of the *old school* approach. Think about early high school basketball teams in their short shorts doing layup drills. Line up, go shoot the layup, repeat. There are no real changes in there, no corrections, just doing that same thing again and again.

Random practice as the name suggests, tends to infuse a few more options into your practice time. There are a couple of cool things that make Random practice interesting.

To start with it simulates *game time* situations more accurately since you are encountering variables just like you would during an actual performance. For example if you are performing sports or a musical concert, there will be slight variations in the heat of the performance compared to how you practice.

Random practice helps you prepare for that by constantly doing something different instead of a simple repetitive movement. It also has the effect of changing things up and having your brain make more small corrections as you go through your practice routine. When you are doing Blocked practice, since you are repeating one movement over and over your brain doesn't have to compute as many variations, or solve new problems, but rather just repeats the exact same thing.

Another interesting thing is that according to researchers, not only will Random practice keep you from getting bored, but the things you are working on will stick with you much better than with Blocked practice.

Richard Schmidt and Tim Lee wrote one of the most researched books on the subject, *Motor Control and Learning: A Behavioral Emphasis.* In it they noted "Skill is retained better following practice under variable conditions."[1]

One of the terms that people who study learning and skill acquisition focus on is "retention". This is important to consider when choosing your practicing methods. You certainly don't want to put in a bunch of time practicing something and then not retain the improvements you made.

So if Random practice gives us more retention than Blocked practice; that's a big deal.

If you have ever been coached you have heard this before. "Do that until you get it right". Or my personal favorite, "Drill it until you can kill it." However it may not be necessary to just do the exact same thing over and over for the best results.

Sometimes the allure of Blocked practice is it *seems* like you are getting it down much better and therefore it makes sense that it should stick with you better and longer. When you do something 20 times in a row, by the 12th time you are starting to feel like you have it, whereas if you are doing it twice and then doing the second movement once and then the third before you go back to the first, it can feel less stable.

However, science is telling us that the Random practice can help you retain skills longer.

Much of this is believed to be due to those small corrections along the way, which have been shown to be an enormously important part of developing skill. Do something, make small corrections, do it again, more corrections, repeat.

Each time you repeat this process you are strengthening the motor skill and reinforcing the brain's neurons and ability to fire off the right signals to perform the skill. The myelin that insulates the nerves in the brain is believed to become stronger each time a skill or movement is performed, and thereby increases the speed and accuracy of the signal.

What is the answer? Should you just drill down on one thing until you get it? Or should you mix things up?

Over the years I have used both methods with success. I don't think this is an either/or situation, but rather a *both* kind of deal.

I think when someone is first learning a skill, Blocked practice helps them get the movement right and focus on small things to make sure they are doing it correctly. Random practice is harder for a beginner as they can either feel like they are never fully getting it, or they can actually develop bad habits since they are not spending as much time dialed in to each movement.

Once a person has the basic skill down and has the movements or sequences correct, then using Random practice can greatly increase their ability to adapt on the fly and be more fluid with their movements. Plus the variations keep it interesting.

Blocked Practice

- Great for the early stages of learning a skill
- Good for building muscle memory as long as you use proper technique

Random Practice

- Proven to be more effective at helping you retain what you practice
- Simulates "game time" by providing more variables
- Keeps practice interesting with more changes

Try mixing up your practice sessions with random variations and see if it doesn't help things stick with you!

9: Chunking

In my early days as a musician, one of my first experiences playing with a band helped show me the importance of *retention*. In particular, it taught me about the dangers of the lack of retention. And even more specifically, how that lack played into our struggle as a band due to the bass player not being able to remember things we had practiced!

We would go over songs and parts many, many times and think we finally had them all down, only to find out the next time we played them the bass player sounded like he had no idea what he was supposed to do. Granted, in his case there could have been some self abuse by the way of occasionally partaking in mind altering substances, but nonetheless it was very annoying to sound like we hadn't practiced when we had!

That showed me the importance of retaining information. It doesn't matter how cool of a practice system you have or how hard you work if you don't remember it later.

There are several ways to remember what we have worked on. Even Norman Bates in Hitchcock's *Psycho* was able to remember his motel guest when pressed by the private investigator. Norman tells us in his nervous stutter, "See now I'm starting to um, ah, remember it. I'm making a mental picture of it in my mind, you know if you make a mental picturization of something…"

Well, he's right. Using mental imagery can help your memory. Visualization, or using *the mind's eye* to help you cement things you want to remember is a great tool. This works for many things we practice. We can take a mental snapshot of the position of our body, or certain movements, or even of the playing or performing surface to help us retain information.

Another technique that will help us take a big step forward in how effectively we retain information and therefore how efficient our practice will be is Chunking. The concept of chunking can be easily understood if we take a look at a random set of letters.

Look at this string of letters for just a few seconds and try to memorize the order. (mrtsa ctciepar)

OK, now without looking back at them can you repeat them? Probably, but you may have had to think for a minute.

Now, lets arrange those exact same letters like this (smart practice).

How long did that take you to memorize the letters involved and the order? That is because you have "chunked" those letters together in a familiar way, you know the words that these letters form, therefore making it easy to recall all of the letters in order.

Chunking several small bits of information together in order to form a larger piece of information which is then memorized is easier than memorizing a large number of unrelated things.

A form of chunking can be found when you make a todo list and have headings such as "phone calls," "emails," "personal tasks." Those lists you create are a way of chunking that information together in an organized fashion.

Using some kind of tool or technique to help you retain information is nothing new. There are many methods that can help you memorize a variety of things. A mnemonic is a learning technique or device that helps you retain information.

Mnemonics come in a variety of flavors. Young musicians memorize the notes on the lines on the staff of the treble clef by saying "Every Good Boy Does Fine." That makes it easy to remember the notes E, G, B, D, F. Or we might use an acronym like HOMES to remember the Great Lakes (Huron, Ontario, Michigan, Erie, Superior), or kids might remember the alphabet by singing the ABC song.

There are a lot of ways to help your memory. The key is to experiment and find ones that work for you. Everyone's brain works a little differently so don't be afraid to try some different methods for remembering your practice material.

For me, when I am practicing, chunking is something that happens more naturally than coming up with an acronym or other methods. If you can learn to chunk information together as you are learning it, you will find that your practice sticks with you much longer.

Chunking is also used in our motor learning, or muscle memory. This is why in the *5 SMART Steps* section of our SMART practice we want to break things down into smaller components. Working on something in several small pieces and then putting those together in a chunk will make it easier to execute and remember.

A couple of key points to help you chunk while you practice:

1. Break things down into smaller pieces.

2. Always look at the relationship between those pieces, this is where you can develop chunks of information that fit together.

3. Constantly experiment with gluing chunks together and then taking them apart. This is how you get down to the fine details of what is working and will undoubtedly help you absorb and retain what you are working on much better!

10: Novelty and Surprise

From the age of 2 all the way through my teen years I spent countless days and nights fishing on the banks of the Raccoon River at Squirrel Hollow park in central Iowa. While there were some memorable times, it was a long time ago and details from various trips are a little hazy. Except for one. I vividly remember sitting next to our blue and white Chevy pickup with my Mom as we heard the news on the radio that Elvis Presley had died. I can remember every little detail about the way the river looked and the fish we caught that day.

This phenomenon of being able to recall details of your surroundings when certain events took place makes for great conversation starters, like "Where were you when X happened." However, what if we inserted *surprise* or what could be considered *novelty* on purpose into our practice routine? What if that could help us remember the details of what we were working on and retain that information? That would be very helpful indeed!

The good news is there is research that shows us just that.

In a research paper called *Absolute Coding of Stimulus Novelty in the Human Substantia Nigra/VTA* that was published in *Neuron* in 2006. - Emrah Düzel, UCL Institute of Cognitive Neuroscience, shared:

"It is a well-known fact amongst scientists that the midbrain region regulates our levels of motivation and our ability to predict rewards by releasing dopamine in the frontal and temporal regions of the brain. We have now shown that novelty activates this brain area. We believe that experiencing novelty might, in itself, have an impact on our dopamine levels."[1]

This study looked at how adding novel or new information in the midst of learning affects memory. The findings confirmed that memory improved with the introduction of novelty.

This is fairly easy to understand without any study as we have all had an experience like I described above where in the midst of something we had done a hundred times, something unusual happened that made us remember that time over the others. The novelty of something different triggered us to remember that.

I have used this technique when working with music students on scales. Running through patterns is not the most fun or interesting thing in the world, which is probably why so many students have difficulty in remembering scale shapes. I found that I could get students to retain these patterns by using a method of novelty during practice. I would have a student run through a scale several times, just straight up and down, and then after a few times I would abruptly stop them in the middle of it and tell them to quickly play a little part of a certain song they knew. I rushed them and made it so they did not have time to think. Then as soon as they played it, I would ask them to resume the scale, and then finish off by playing the scale once more.

Besides crazy looks from students the first time I would do this, I also noticed that without any more work, they seemed to have the scale down much more solid than they did by just repeating the scale. I would occasionally do this with students regardless of what they were learning - interrupt and have them quickly play something unrelated and then get back to the task at hand. I also think not knowing whether or not I was going to have them do something else in the middle of their scale made them concentrate more. Plus, as they would remember the last time I did that to them they would remember what I had them play then, and this memory seemed to "overlap" into memory of the scale. Like supercharging the memory.

This obviously can have huge implications on getting better at something as being able to ramp up your memory allows you to keep key concepts and techniques sharp.

In one of Dr. Duzel's experiments he had subjects look at pictures as they flashed by. Some subjects saw pictures repeated, and for some subjects they added in new unusual pictures they saw only once. The interesting thing they found was that learning and memory "is more effective if you mix new facts in with the old, you actually learn better, even though your brain is also tied up with new information. Subjects performed best in these tests when new information was combined with familiar information during learning. After a 20 minute delay, subjects' memory for slightly familiar information was boosted by 19 percent if it had been mixed with new facts during learning sessions."

A 19% increase is a major leap if you are trying to retain all the information you can about your practice session!

How can we use this information to practice smarter? How can we implement techniques in our practice routines to stimulate that dopamine release?

1. See things in a new way.

Just looking at your environment in a new way can trigger some novelty in your practicing sessions. If you are working on your golf swing at the driving range, take a minute and notice something that you haven't before. Maybe it is the way the far fence looks like it is crooked, maybe it is the lights above you and how they haven't been cleaned! Whatever it is, just make a note of it and really focus on it for a few seconds and then get back to practicing. It has to be something you haven't thought of or noticed before. This jolt of new thinking can actually kick that dopamine in and help your retention.

2. Do something crazy!

Practicing can be tedious, mentally draining, and as mentioned become redundant at times. So we occasionally need a real shock to feel like we are being shaken back into the now. One way to step it up is in the middle of practicing, do something crazy and fun. It doesn't have to be related to what you are practicing on, as a matter of fact it should be completely different! If you are practicing piano, jump up and do a cartwheel - if you are working on chess, stand up and sing your favorite song as loud as you possibly can - if you are practicing pitching a baseball, stop and walk like a duck all the way to home plate. Get weird! That is novelty at it's finest! That will make what you do memorable, break up the monotony and boost your retention of the skills you are learning and practicing!

From what I have witnessed and what science tells us, there are good reasons to add a little novelty and surprise to your practice sessions!

11: Getting Good at Being Bad

One of the biggest challenges we face on our quest to get better can be caused by practicing! What? Wait a minute! Practicing is a good thing right? Well, not if you are practicing something over and over again, but doing it wrong. All this does is make you really good at being really bad!

Motor learning, or what we often refer to as muscle memory is the ability to repeat a movement to the point where it doesn't require conscious effort. This is what helps a tennis player throw the ball way over their head and in one smooth motion jump and swing their racket for a serve hitting the ball precisely. Or what allows a piano player to get down fast and difficult passages, seemingly playing faster than the brain could possibly think, all the while hitting the right notes. It's even what lets us get up out of our easy chair and walk to the kitchen to fill the coffee cup!

If we had to consciously think of any of those movements it would make them very difficult. By practicing and repeating something many times, it becomes automatic.

But here's the thing about motor learning. Muscle memory doesn't discriminate between good and bad technique. It will learn and retain bad technique just the same as it will good technique. So if you are practicing something wrong, you are just strengthening and reinforcing the wrong way to do it. Each time you practice something the wrong way, you lay another brick in the wall that stands between you and getting better.

Remember how the myelin around nerves builds with each repetition of a task increasing the speed of the impulses? Once again, that is the same thing here, every time you do something wrong you are just building up that nerve connection to make it easier and faster to do it wrong again.

We all know how hard it is to make a change or break a bad habit. Orison Swett Marden said, "The beginning of a habit is like an invisible thread, but every time we repeat the act we strengthen the strand, add to it another filament, until it becomes a great cable and binds us irrevocably, thought and act." I agree with most of that, although I actually believe we can break that bind, but it is not easy.

Studies on exactly how many times it takes doing something to "get it down" are difficult to conduct. You can isolate one movement and study that, but it is hard to say it will take you X amount of repetitions to perfect shooting a free throw in basketball. The complexity in your motor skills when you have multiple movements or segments makes it hard to isolate and measure each area. It is difficult to predict how many times you need to practice Bach's *Bouree in Em* on guitar before you have it in your muscle memory due to all the various things that are happening as you play it. You will hear lots of numbers as you read through literature on the subject; 600 times, 1000 times, 10,000 times. So many variables come into play with each different skill that it makes an exact universal number impossible.

However, what is true is that studies have shown that it takes at least 3 to 5 times MORE repetitions to unlearn something and then relearn it the right way once you have it down wrong. So if we are talking about thousands of repetitions, that makes it pretty easy to see the benefit of learning things right the first time.

How can we avoid this problem of practicing the wrong things, and developing bad habits on our way to getting better?

The old carpenter's adage, "Measure twice, cut once" can be implemented here. Make sure you are doing things the right way before you start repeating it.

This is why I emphasize having an organized and systematic practice plan. One that will encourage you to constantly track, analyze and review what and how you are practicing. Even with things that you think you have down, don't take them for granted! Go back through things you have been doing for years and look at all movement, posture, level of relaxation, and more. Really TRY to find what is wrong. Even if it is a small thing, fix it now! The sooner you fix something that you find is wrong, the less time it will take to get it back on track moving in the right direction. Finding and repairing these little things will elevate your overall level.

One good method for dealing with this is to do what I call a "Spring cleaning" practice session every couple of months. This is where you will do nothing but look at all of the things you already think you know, and try to be extra critical to see if they can be improved. If you find something you need to work on, put it back on the "What I am working on" list so you can get it back on the schedule.

It can be hard to admit you are doing something wrong when you have invested a lot of time into it already. Just realize that certain things can continue to get stronger and make things worse if you let them go, so dig in and fix it now!

12: Gamification

When I was a little kid we had a pool table. However, as an only child, when my Dad was at work I had nobody to play with. So, I would practice, but found that I stayed more interested if I made up various games. I would sometimes just play as two players, switching cue sticks as each "player" took their turn. But often I would create new games; Set three balls in the center and see how many shots it took to make them all. Then keep trying to better my score.

Back then that was just considered a kid entertaining himself, nowadays that would be called *gamification*.

Gamification is everywhere. There are books written about it, you can take courses to learn the finer points of it, and hire consultants to help you implement it into every aspect of your business or life.

Basically, gamification is the practice of applying game mechanics to non-game situations. So if you take a website where you want more engagement from visitors, you could create a game that rewards people for finding hidden pictures, and gives them a gold badge each time they find one.

People like to play games. We all like the challenge of making it to the next level, keeping score and seeing how our score stacks up against others. We like incentives and rewards.

The studies that support the effectiveness of gamification are plentiful. Gamification has been shown to work in areas from technology and marketing, to personal development and education.

The idea of incentives is not new. It has been around since prehistoric man was incentivized to run fast to keep from becoming lunch for T-Rex.

Can we use gamification to successfully make our practice more effective? Absolutely! The real key is to think about it ahead of time and actually map out how some sections of our practice will be a *game*.

I think the most effective use of gaming during practice can be found in anything that helps you reinforce something that you need in your skill. Perhaps you are looking to develop a better setup to your tennis serve, so making a game out of that part of your practice will help. When I am working on my Frisbee throw I often take 30 discs out and then see how many I can throw into a defined circle in the field. I then try to beat that score with another round. It makes the practice more fun, and I am developing that skill I need.

Gamification can be as simple as that, or more involved such as logging your success and giving yourself some type of reward for each milestone you hit. Once again, you are trying to condition or reinforce a behavior during practice that will translate to the skill.

The concepts of *Reinforcement* and *Conditioning* were explored in depth by American psychologist B.F. Skinner. The way Skinner explained the concept of reinforcement was: Behavior which is reinforced tends to be repeated, behavior which is not reinforced tends to fade away.

So using any technique we can to reinforce a desirable behavior will pay off in the long run. Set your practice up with some sort of gamification elements to reinforce the behaviors you want to build.

I worked with a golfer who would give himself a little gold star sticker in his practice journal on the days he hit X number of balls exactly where he wanted on the driving range. He basically rewarded himself when he achieved the goal that he had setup. While this might seem simple, when he looked back at the monthly calendar he could easily see the gold stars. What it did for him was give him a snapshot and a reinforcement that his practice was working.

This visualization of his gold star success both fed the "gamer" inside of him (he could see his achievements and likely wanted to get more gold stars next month) and at the same time created this behavior (hit X amount of balls where he wanted) that was reinforced by seeing the success of it - which according to Skinner would make him more likely to want to repeat it. Basically a win all the way around.

If what we are practicing is a game in itself, we can sometimes just think that is enough. However, usually in practice we are not playing the entire game. We are not playing an entire soccer match or doing a full baseball game. We just work on parts. So we still need to "gamify" the parts that we are working on.

If you find yourself bogged down during practice, creating a game can give you a lift and actually shift your focus away from the drudgery and on to something fun. Be creative! Know that when it comes to practice, playing games is still serious business!

13: Premack That

Pink Floyd put it quite profoundly: "You can't have any pudding if you don't eat your meat."

They probably didn't realize they were espousing the Premack principle, or that this wisdom could be used for training and advancing skills of all sorts.

Psychology Professor David Premack studied and wrote extensively about reinforcement. His breakthrough theory about reinforcement was later referred to as the *Premack Principle.*

The basic premise of this is that a person will do a less preferred activity in order to get to do a more preferred activity.

For example, you might want to eat the pudding (more preferred activity), but are not crazy about eating the meat (less preferred activity). However, you know what the song says, "You can't have any pudding unless you eat your meat." Therefore you go ahead and do that less preferred activity of meat eating because doing that will then unlock the opportunity to partake in the more preferred pudding fest!

While eating may seem to be a stretch when we are thinking of activities, we can find this same idea in other areas.

Premacking is sometimes a buzzword in dog training. Here is how it might work. My dog loves to go chase a ball after I throw it. I want him to do this for exercise, so it is an activity we both desire. However, I need him to first pickup the ball and hand it to me so I can throw it. This activity is not much fun for him so he is not that excited about doing it (he has to give up control of the ball, acquiesce to my authority, and come to me when he would rather just run around).

But, those are all things that I want him to do. He knows that by doing the activity of giving me the ball, (the less preferred activity), then the result will be I throw the ball and he chases it, (more preferred). So I am building the activity of handing me the ball by rewarding or reinforcing with the activity of letting him chase it.

Basically we are using an activity to reinforce another activity. Instead of just using a treat to reward a behavior.

Let's say you are a golfer, and you love to go out and just smash big drives, shooting for max distance. Now you need to practice that, so it is not a bad thing, but you know you also really should be working on sinking 5 foot putts. The old adage "Drive for show, putt for dough," keeps creeping into your mind.

Well, the way to Premack this is to make yourself sink 20 of those 5 foot putts before you allow yourself to whack the long ball. This way you work on both things and eventually you will accept the importance of making those putts for their own sake.

You can also put a series of skills together this way.

For example if you are a guitarist, and you want to do the desirable activity of improvising or jamming over a blues song, you may want to build a series of warm ups that lead to that.

First you have to play your Major Scale shape 5 times. Once that is done you will cycle through a series of cool sounding chord forms. Then you play through a fun picking exercise and THEN you do the jam over the song. So each new thing is more desirable or fun than the last thing and it all leads up to the ultimate payoff of jamming!

This is similar to another term we often hear called *back-chaining*. Basically starting with the end result you hope to achieve, but then going backwards through each step it took to get there and working on those steps individually. This is not as much about using a more desirable activity to reinforce a less desirable one as it is just building a skill. But they can look similar at times.

Consider taking some time to see if what you are practicing can benefit from the Premack Principle. Try it on a couple of things and see if it doesn't help you reinforce that thing you are not crazy about doing.

Just remember that practice can be broken down and organized just like any activity in life. You wake up and it's a beautiful day. You really want to go out to the park and play. But you look around and your room is a mess. You tell yourself first you have to clean your room, then you can go to the park. Congratulations, you have just Premacked your day!

14: Three Ps

Whatever skill you want to get better at, it helps to look at it through the filter of the *3 Ps.*

Each time you partake in the activity you want to improve, you are doing one of these three things. Which one of these you focus on the most, and invest the most time in will determine how you excel. So let's take a look at the three Ps.

Three Ps

1. **Play**
2. **Profit**
3. **Practice**

1. Play. This happens each time you do it just for fun. For example if you want to get better at guitar you may pick up your guitar and just mess around. You might play some songs for a friend, jam to your favorite T.V. Commercial, or play around with a new effects pedal. Or if Tennis is the skill you are working on, playing may involve a casual game, or just hitting some balls against a wall. There is nothing wrong with this first "P", as a matter of fact it is an essential part of life! Having fun is often the very reason you want to get better at a particular skill in the first place! So it is good to relax and have some fun and just "play" occasionally. After all, as Mr. Torrance taught us from his typewriter at the historic Overlook Hotel, "All work and no play makes Jack a dull boy."

We all know someone who has attempted the path to improvement just by making use of this first "P". An example is the golfer who wants to get better and their way to achieve that is by just playing a couple of rounds every other weekend with their buddies. While it certainly is possible to get better at something to some degree just by doing it over and over, it's not the best way. To start with, it will likely take you much longer by not having a plan that helps you determine what you really need to work on next. The other huge problem with this method is that without a plan, you will probably develop bad habits, and may actually create technique troubles that can completely stall your progress.

This first P is where I see many people get frustrated. They sometimes spend years just playing, and get frustrated because they haven't gotten much better. They get tricked by the illusion that since they are putting in lots of hours doing the skill, they should be getting good. When they don't see much real progress, they sometimes think they "just aren't cutout for this," and they quit caring, quit trying, or just plain quit!

2. Profit. Every activity may not have as apparent of a "profit" time, but if you are a drummer and doing a gig - this is "profit" time. If you are working on your basketball game, the "profit" time would be when you are playing a game with your local YMCA team. Profit time does not have to actually involve you making money at it, but you are doing something that is not exclusively for your own enjoyment or advancement. This is any time you do your activity for *work*, or in *have to* mode. Like our first P - Play - you can get better each time you do your activity for profit. For example if you are playing in a band that is doing 6 nights a week in a club - that is a lot of playing and certain aspects of your skill development will benefit from that. If you are trying to improve your computer coding, and you take a gig writing some code for a project, you will get better to some degree, however, most "Profit" opportunities don't require you to push yourself to the edge or try new things. In fact, it is usually just the opposite - do what is required - do it safe - do it right.

As we'll see later, this safe mode is detrimental to real advancement in your skill. The way you get better is by pushing the boundaries. Coloring inside the lines will always make a nice picture, but coloring outside the lines is how you discover and create something new! When you want to see dramatic improvement, you eventually have to stretch.

3. Practice. I define practice as *"Doing activities specifically designed for the purpose of improving performance in an organized and* *systematic way."* Read that again. "Doing activities specifically designed for the purpose of improving performance". This is practice with intention… SMART practice.

When you actually practice something instead of just doing it for play or profit, you have a different mindset. You are expecting to improve, and you know what you need to do in order to make that happen. Having that shift in your perception may seem like a small difference, but it can have a huge impact!

Now I want you to take a look at anything you have tried to get better at over the years. Pick any skill you have worked on, and I would bet that if you have struggled to improve or have gotten frustrated, you can probably trace that back to spending too much time in the first "P" - Play. That is the most common place to see skill improvement flounder. Between the fun of playing, and the illusion it gives you of (time = getting better), our first P is a slippery slope we have to navigate on our path to real improvement.

The right formula isn't "time = getting better", but rather it's "time spent practicing the right things in the right way = getting better". I know, it doesn't roll off the tongue quite as nicely, but the results it will give you will more than make up for that!

The surest way to improve is to spend the majority of your time in the third P - Practice. That is where you will see the biggest gains and the most efficient and effective improvement.

Whenever you look at something you are trying to improve, take some time to think about which "P" you are spending the most time in, and adjust accordingly.

15: SMART Practice Triangle

Need a confidence boost before you dig in? Not sure if you can get better? Wondering if practice will really payoff?

I'm about to give you the best news in the world if you're looking to get better at anything. Ready?

I have NEVER seen anyone who practiced the right things, in the right way, and put in the time, NOT get better! Period! So rejoice! This means you not only *can* get better, but if you apply these principles you *will* get better.

This is like a natural law, something that simply works. Like the law of the harvest, you reap what you sow. You don't plant apple seeds and get peaches. Likewise if you follow the SMART Practice Triangle you will see positive results.

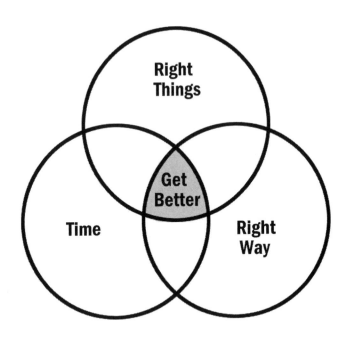

So let's take a look at the three elements you need in order for getting better to be a sure thing:

Practice the right things. This seems like it should be pretty obvious, but often we don't get clear on what those right things are. If you want to build up your biceps and all you do is squats, that is not going to get you to where you want to be. Or if your desire is to get better at putting in your golf game, but when you have some time all you do is go out and try to crush long drives, that will not help. So you have to look at and assess what are the things you need to do for this particular skill that will help propel you to where you want to be.

The *Skillbox Inventory* can really help you figure out what the right things are. Doing the Inventory will show you what you are now doing, and what you need to do in order to bridge the gap between where you are and where you want to be.

Practice the right way. Once you know what things you should be working on, you still have to do them in the right way or you will fail. This is where most people stumble and what causes the most frustration for people who fall short of getting the results they want.

Working on things the right way can be accomplished by using the *SMART Practice scheduler* to map out your practice sessions, and then working with the *5 SMART Steps* to breakdown and work on each skill.

Put in the time. Once you know the right things to practice, and have figured out the right way to practice them, you then have to put the time into doing them to see results.

There is some variability built into the time corner of the Triangle. You can think of "putting in the time" as a sliding scale to some degree. If you put in a little time, you will get a little better. If you want to get a lot better, you may have to slide that time scale to the right and put in a little more time.

The key to any triangle is having all three corners. The same holds true for our SMART Practice Triangle. It only works when all three are present.

If you know exactly what the right things are to practice, and you know how to do them in the right way, but don't put in the time… it won't work. If you know those right things and have a ton of time to work on them, but don't do them in the right way… you won't see any improvement. Finally, if you know the right way to work on things and are able to put in the time, but are working on the wrong things to start with… you are not going to get better.

You have to practice the right things, in the right way, and put in the time, and then you will see the improvement you are looking for.

If you only solidify one thought in your mind about

practice, one mantra that you tell yourself over and over again, make it this.

"If I practice the right things, in the right way, and put in the time, I WILL get better!"

Part Three: SMART Practice Core System

16: **Intro to System**

When I'm speaking in front of a group of people, I often ask if anyone has anything that they are trying to get better at doing. The hands shoot up enthusiastically. Then I ask if any of those who raised their hands have more than one thing they would like to get better at. Almost all of the hands stay up. Then I follow that up with the question, "Do you have a specific plan to improve each of those things, are you following that plan, and is it working?" Hands go down and I usually hear crickets.

The fact is that most of us have not only one thing, but multiple things in our lives that we would like to be better at, but we don't have a definite plan in place to help us move forward for each thing. This leads to wishing and dreaming of being better, but not getting there.

How can we expect to improve without having a plan of action to help us do so? Maybe we are hoping that as we mature we will gain some kind of magical wisdom that will help us understand the way to improvement.

Action is what will get you on the path to improvement. Leonardo DaVinci said "I have been impressed with the urgency of doing, knowing is not enough, we must apply, being willing is not enough, we must do." Well, Leo was a guy who certainly had a knack for getting better at a lot of things so he must have been on to something!

The reality is, it is foolish to think we can get better at things without a plan and a system of action in place to propel us forward. We wouldn't set out on a road trip without a GPS or a map. We wouldn't start to build a house without a blueprint. Heck we wouldn't even try to put together a ready-to-assemble bookcase without printed instructions. And yet, we find ourselves with many things we want to get better at, and no plan to show us how.

To paraphrase Newton's first law of motion; An object set in motion tends to stay in motion – and an object that just sits on the couch…. Well, you get the idea. We need motion, we need to get up and take action and develop a plan! Not only will having an organized system of practice help you get better – it will help you get better faster, more efficiently, and with less errors that could potentially derail your progress. As an added bonus, if you take less time to get better at one thing, that means you'll have time leftover to get better at something else!

Some of the first steps when setting out to improve should include taking stock in where you are and what you already know. I am constantly surprised when I work with someone who wants to improve something, and ask them to tell me "What they already know." They usually say "I don't know much." However, when we start unpacking that, I find out they know quite a bit, but it is usually just not organized into a system they can readily access. It's just floating around randomly in their head. Once we organize it and then step back and look at all they know about that particular subject they are always amazed they know more than they thought. So once we get into the SMART Practice system, looking at exactly where you are will really help you plot out your path of where you are going.

The SMART practice core system is comprised of 4 parts; Skill Goal, Skillbox Inventory, SMART Zone Schedule, and the 5 SMART Steps.

SMART Practice Core System

1. Skill Goal
2. Skillbox Inventory
3. SMART Zone Schedule
4. 5 SMART Steps

The absolute best way to work through the system is to start at the beginning and go through each section. You will find that each section builds on the work you did in the last and creates a complete plan. However, you may decide that you just need to get better at scheduling your time, and you can go directly to the SMART Zone practice section to dig into that. Or if you already know what you need to do, have a pretty good schedule set up, but just need to get a grasp on how to work on the specific parts, then check out the 5 SMART Steps.

However you choose to apply the different parts of the system is up to you. Just know that the SMART Practice System has worked for many, many people helping them get better at a variety of skills. The tools are here, so jump in and get better!

17: Skill Goal: System Part 1

Alice asked, "Which way should I go?" The wise Cheshire Cat responded by asking her, "Where do you want to get to?" Alice replied, "I don't much care." To which the Cat answered, "Then it doesn't matter which way you go."

Just like Alice in *Alice's Adventures in Wonderland*, if you don't get clear on where you want to go, it won't matter how much time you put in or what you practice.

Working out your *Skill Goal* is the first step of the SMART Practice core system, and is much like the first step of any journey or undertaking. We want to determine where we are going. Knowing where you are going not only motivates you, keeps you focused and on track, but can also play a huge role in selecting exactly what material you will be working on. We can think of this as setting a goal, but I really like to think of it more as laying out the *destination* of where you want to get in this skill.

While it is fine to spend a little time thinking about this, I imagine you probably have a good idea of where you want to take the skill you are working on, so you can just start with that. It may change as you progress. You may start out just wanting to improve a little, and then as you find yourself getting better, you may decide to keep going.

Let's say you want to improve your bowling game. You may just be starting out and you want to learn the basics so you can bowl with friends a couple times a year. Or maybe you already bowl a couple times a year and you actually want to beat those friends! You might be interested in getting good enough to join a local league and roll with "The Dude", or you might want to step it up and win that league! You might even want to hit the road on the Pro Bowlers Tour! The point is, write down the level you want to get to. You don't have to know exactly *how* you will do it, we'll figure that out, but start with what you are shooting for with this skill.

Not having a clear idea of where you are going, or exact steps for getting there can lead to frustration with your practice. Many people just sort of float along, working on bits of this and that and hoping somehow they just happen to improve in the right direction. The way to fix that mistake is to first determine where you want to end up, and then put together a specific practice plan to take you there.

Just like setting goals for anything in your life, individual goals for skills can be comprised of short term and long term goals. It is often good to set your long term goals first and then work backwards in time to figure out the steps you will need to take to get there.

If I am working with a guitar student, I might ask them to identify their goal. Do you want to just play a few chords, learn some strums so you can sit around the campfire with friends and sing some songs? Or, do you want to become a virtuoso and an in demand studio session player who has amazing skills?

They might ask, "But why do I need to figure out my goal? If I want to be a better guitar player can't I just head in that direction?"

There are a couple of schools of thought on this. The first one adheres to the following general way of thinking. Say you are climbing a mountain but you are not sure how far you want to go. Wouldn't you just head for the top on the same trail and in the same way that the person who is going to the peak is going? You could basically follow their footsteps but just stop when you get as far as you want to go. Wouldn't the techniques and skills needed to get to the top serve you along the way as well?

This sounds plausible, but let's look at another option.

The second method for tackling the mountain goes more like this. Set your first goal as getting to the foothills. Then once there, if you want to go on, your next goal would maybe be the basecamp halfway up the mountain. If you get there, you may decide to set a goal of reaching the peak.

Why this second way of setting smaller incremental goals may actually make more sense, is that many of the skills and processes needed to reach the peak may not be necessary to just get to the foothills for a simple hike. If you are going all the way to the top, you might need a completely different set of gear; ropes, packs, supplies, even oxygen. You also may need a different set of skills to reach the peak, which might require more specific and longer training.

If your goal is just to hike up to the foothills you would be wasting time working on the specific skills and knowledge that are only needed for those going to the peak.

Back to our guitar student who just wants to sing songs around the campfire, some of the techniques and knowledge needed to become a virtuoso will just end up frustrating her and make her want to give up. It is a different amount of work and dedication to become a virtuoso. Why burden someone with that when they just want to get a little bit better?

I think this second method works better for most of us because the reality is, for most of the things we want to get better at, we are not looking to become the best in the world, we just want to get a little better. Now if your goal is to be the best, then by all means set your aim high. But if you are just trying to learn some campfire songs, practicing scales for 2 hours a day may not be your best use of time!

You will certainly find some of the principles and abilities needed to excel at a skill are universal and necessary regardless of your goals, but some things will be different depending on how far you want to go.

That is why we want to consider our goal and look at where we are trying to take the skill we are setting out to improve. That way we can make sure we are working on exactly what we need during our practice time.

When you set your goal for the skill, remember, it can change. Maybe we start out and just want to play a few songs around the campfire. But then once you accomplish that you may think, "Hey, it would be pretty cool to be able to play in a band." After you get a taste of playing in a band, you might think, "Wouldn't it be great if I could make a living playing music!" That will bring you to a new set of skills you need. So by setting the first destination, you are creating the building blocks to everything else you will do.

The other real benefit of setting these smaller incremental goals is that they seem attainable! The goal of climbing to the top of the mountain can seem so daunting and far off, that many get frustrated, impatient and quit. But the goal of making it to that first step creates motion and momentum. It's the *action* that we talked about needing to take to improve anything!

Get moving! That is the key.

The important thing is to look at what you want to do with this skill so you can start to assemble the pieces needed to put into your practice routine in order to get you to that first target.

We started this section out with wisdom from a cat, so we'll end with some from a man who gave us an amazing *Cat in the Hat.*

Congratulations!
Today is your day.
You're off to Great Places!
You're off and away!
You have brains in your head.
You have feet in your shoes
You can steer yourself
Any direction you choose.

The action you need to take for step 1 of the SMART Practice system is easy. Simply think through and write down your goal for this skill.

18: Skillbox Inventory: System Part 2

When I was a little kid I had a toybox, a place for all my stuff. I remember occasionally dumping it all out in the middle of the floor to do an inventory of sorts, basically taking stock of my world.

I would create three piles. In the first pile were the toys I knew well. I knew the names of all the little action figures, I knew what all the little cars would do, and which toys went in which category. In the second pile were the toys that I was working on. Basically anything that I didn't really know that well, maybe they were new and I didn't have all their moves down, or maybe it was just a new addition to the "army guys" who didn't have a name or a job in the regiment yet. You could also find cars with missing wheels or a house with a missing door - things that needed some work. The third pile wasn't really a pile as much as it was a list. It was like a Christmas list of the toys I needed to complete my toybox. These were the ones I didn't have yet, but I was sure that if I got them they would enhance my toybox.

When I grew up and started to develop the SMART Practice system and needed a way to help me assess my current level of skill and knowledge on something I was trying to get better at, the toybox seemed like the perfect analogy.

So I created a technique I call the *Skillbox Inventory*. I am a believer in compartmentalizing the info related to each skill you are trying to get better at. Instead of just having a brain full of a million different bits of info related to all the different things you are trying to improve, we will organize it into sections so it is easier to focus on what you need to do for each particular skill you are practicing.

Taking a Skillbox Inventory is similar to dumping out your toybox.

Productivity guru David Allen in *Getting Things Done* talks about performing a "Brain Dump" of everything you need to do in order to be able to better organize your tasks. That is what I want you to do with all of your knowledge regarding the skill you are organizing a practice plan for.

Start out by creating 3 lists. This is where you will organize all of the info pertaining to your skill. We will use the things from these lists when we make out our SMART Zone schedule, so make sure you do these lists as it's a crucial part of the system!

Label your three lists with these headings:

1. What I know
2. What I'm working on
3. What I need to know

1. What I know. The size of this first list will vary depending on if you are just starting to work on this skill, or if you have been doing it for years. You may have been playing piano for 10 years and just now have decided to organize your practice time. This list will be quite large for you. You may want to divide this list up into sub-sections. If you are that piano player you might have sections on scales, chords, songs, exercises and more. You need to write down every single thing you already know here. Even if it seems trivial, write it down.

You don't have to be a master of everything here, but you should know it without stopping or thinking about what you are doing. This is all the stuff about this skill that you know. If you have something that you know pretty well, but it still needs some work, don't put it here. It will go in the next list. This list is for things you feel comfortable that you know.

Getting this list done is actually a powerful thing in itself because chances are, whether you are a beginner or expert, you probably know more than you thought you did. Seeing it written down helps you feel like you're moving forward. This list along with the next one forms the main *inventory* of all you know or are working on.

2. What I'm working on. This list will change the most because as you get these things down they will move to the *What I know* list, and you will be replenishing this list with things from the following list of what you need to know. This list should be full of all the things you have started to tackle, but don't know completely yet, or things that you just haven't put in enough time on to feel you "know" them.

3. What I need to know. This is the list of things you will need to know and be able to do in order to take your skill to the next level. If you are just starting out, you may have a little difficulty with this list, because you might not be sure exactly what you need to know! This is where it is helpful to have an instructor help you drill down on the next things you will need to work on. You can also consult your master goals list to help you with this. As a matter of fact, many of your short term goal items can be on this list. But, you are not really prioritizing or organizing them here, just listing stuff you need to be able to do to get better.

What I Know	What I'm Working On	What I Need to Know

Once you have your three lists written out, you need to review them often to stay abreast of your path and progress. These lists are what you will use to plan your practice schedule.

This circle of knowledge will provide a fluid learning path; the things from *What I'm working on* eventually move onto the *What I know* list. The *What I need to know* list will feed the *What I'm working on* list.

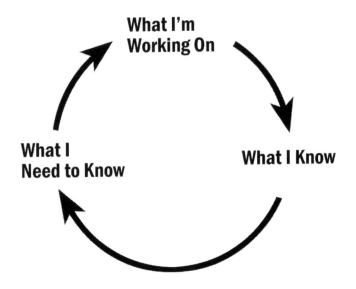

Depending on what you are practicing and your skill level, you may find some overlap within your lists. For example if you are practicing tennis, in the *What I know* list you might write down that you know how to serve. But in the *What I'm working on* list you may have down that you are working on developing a better serve. Maybe you need more speed, accuracy and consistency. You just have to remember that some things from list 1 will be things you will also continue to work on and tweak so variations may end up in list 2.

One of the biggest benefits of making these lists will be the ability to see an overall snapshot of where you are. You can see both where you are and where you are going all in one spot. It is really hard to see everything clearly when it is all jumbled together in that grey matter in your skull. But when you can lay it all out in the three lists you can step back and get a great overview. Take it out of the grey matter and put it on the white paper.

Russell Wilson said, "The separation is in the preparation."

That is very true even when it comes to preparing to practice! Many times when we decide to practice something we just head to the field or the court, grab our instrument, open our writing pad, start rehearsing our speech, or get ourselves immediately to whatever our practice environment may be and dig right in.

However, taking the time to map out and organize your practice material ahead of time will pay big dividends. Doing the Skillbox Inventory gives you a really clear and complete picture of all the elements of the skill you want to get better at. Then you'll be ready to take the next step and schedule your actual practice time with things that have been specifically chosen to move you forward.

19: SMART Zone Schedule: System Part 3

Now that you have determined your goals and have done the Skillbox Inventory, you have a great foundation to build your practice on. This brings us to the next part of our plan, where we schedule our actual practice time.

You should have the 3 lists in front of you that were created when you did the Skillbox Inventory. You are going to use the material from those lists to fill out the SMART Zone practice schedule.

I find that dividing practice time into too many sections can make things confusing. Too many moving parts can keep us from following through on the plan. So I like to stick with 3 sections or *zones* of practice.

I want you to divide whatever time you have to practice into 3 zones. Regardless of whether you have 30 minutes or 3 hours to practice, we will divide that time into 3 zones. Zone 1 is 10 to 20% of your time, Zone 2 is 60 to 80%, and Zone 3 is 10 to 20%. This doesn't have to be exact but we roughly want Zone 2 to have a bigger chunk of time, so a 1 hour practice session could be 40 to 50 minutes in Zone 2 with Zones 1 and 3 splitting the rest.

Once your time has been divided up, let's look at what to actually practice in each of these zones.

Zone 1: Warm Ups and Drills

This zone is where you get your head in the game. Get yourself situated. It's the deep breath before the plunge. Start slow by doing things you are very familiar with. You will do warm ups, or drills, going over the basics. If you are playing guitar, here is where you will do some exercises and simple songs that get you warmed up. If you are practicing your golf game, here is where you do some basic stretching and warming up with a few swings. You might go through your technique slowly here and focus on proper form.

The material you will work on here will definitely be stuff you pull from your *What I know* list. This isn't stuff you are still working on or new stuff you are learning, but rather things you have down. How many items you will put in this zone depends on how much time you have for this practice session. If you only have a short time to practice then just pull a couple of things from the *What I know* list and put them here in Zone 1. If you have a longer time to practice you might pull another one or two.

Before you leave Zone 1, do a little mental self encouragement. Remind yourself that now you are prepared to go into Zone 2 and the stuff you are going to work on there will make big improvements for you. Always keep your thinking focused and positive when you practice. That will lead to getting the most benefit from your practice time!

Zone 2: Learning and Working

Here is where we will spend the bulk of our practice time. This zone is where we really push our skill forward. The things we put in this zone to work on will come from our *What I'm working on* list. This is stuff that you are currently practicing on and don't yet have it to the level you would like. You may also pull something new from the "What I need to know" list and start digging into it. This is the part of the system that helps you get into new things in an organized and trackable way. Spend a few minutes at the end of this zone's time to review notes from your practice notebook and make sure you are seeing the progress you want.

Same thing as in Zone 1, how many things you put here will depend on how much time you have. You can just put a couple of things in here if they really need drilling down on. Even if you have more time, be mindful of overwhelming this list with too many things. Start with fewer and see what you get accomplished. Remember, this zone is focused work.

Zone 3: Playing and Creating

This zone is the payoff for all the work you did in the previous two zones! I find that having small rewards at the end of each practice session makes practice seem less like work and more like fun! Playing and creating seem normal if you are practicing music, but what about other things? Absolutely. If you are practicing basketball and working on shooting free throws in Zone 2, in Zone 3 you might step back to do some Meadowlark Lemon style hook shots from half court! Or you might shoot with your other hand, or you might shoot 3 then do a handstand! Make it fun. Make it creative! If you are practicing speaking German, in this zone you may try to pick 6 words and say them out of order as fast as you can. Laugh. Have fun. Make the end of your practice a really light hearted fun time!

The business of practice takes place in the first two zones. However, you still can be learning in Zone 3. You may find that when you loosen up and just have fun with something, that is where you see some real breakthroughs. Remember, just because you are having fun doesn't mean you are not potentially tapping into some real benefit for your skill!

You can do things in Zone 3 from your first two lists, or you can just create and make up stuff here. Write down a couple of things to do in Zone 3, but stay flexible. The key is that it has to be enjoyable and adventurous!

Unfortunately, without having a system and doing a little planning, many people start their practice time in Zone 3 and never leave there. That might be fun, but getting stuck there won't move you forward like being more organized will.

After you finish filling out Zone 3, you will have your practice time planned out. Your practice will then be structured like this:

- 2 to 4 things from your *What I know* list in Zone 1.
- Then 2 to 4 things listed in Zone 2 that you pulled from your *What I'm working on* list.
- Finally in Zone 3 you will have a couple of things from any of your lists, or just have some free time listed to do some experimenting!

It should be pointed out that while this division of time should be the normal way you schedule your practice, keep in mind that you can vary this if you need to. For example: You may have an hour to practice and after a few minute of drills you just want to be creative. Fine - spend 10 minutes on drills and the rest of the time just jamming. Or you may be frustrated with a particular aspect of your technique and decide to spend the whole hour just woodshedding on that. This is great! The key is you should always be aware of what you are working on, and make a conscious effort to plan your time. As long as most of your practice sessions have you working with the structure of the 3 SMART Zones, occasionally changing up what you do during practice is fine. Starting with these zones will get you on track and keep a balance between what you already know and what you need to know.

Taking time to plan each practice session will make a huge difference in how effective you are at practice. Just wasting time and being unclear on what you should do when you start to practice is a progress killer. Get specific! If you do this each time you practice, you can mix it up with a wide variety of things and keep practice fun. Pulling things from your Skillbox Inventory lists also helps you constantly review the various things you need to work on. Many times I have had people say, "Yeah, I forgot to work on that". So looking back at your lists and picking things for each practice session keeps it all in the loop.

Of course when you really need to focus on something, you can keep it in your schedule for however long it takes to get it down. This SMART Zone scheduling method gives you the best of both worlds; variety to keep it interesting, and pinpoint focus to really nail stuff.

20: SMART Steps: System Part 4

Now we've set our goals, done the Skillbox Inventory, divided up our time and moved items from our lists into the 3 SMART Zones on the schedule. How do we actually go about working on the material in order to get the most out of it? We want to be effective with our practice time and make sure the time we spend produces good results.

The SMART practice system of working on anything should contain these 5 SMART steps. When you tackle a skill with these steps you will see exceptional results and improvement.

Here are the 5 SMART steps:

1. You gotta want it - Have the mindset that you are motivated to practice this for the sole purpose to improve.

2. Analyze the skill to be practiced and break it down into small parts.

3. Work on these parts individually using various techniques.

4. Put the small parts together and work on the whole, again using various techniques.

5. Analyze and track your effectiveness along the way. Get feedback from an instructor, or self analysis by using the *Four R Circle*. (Check out the chapter on the Four R Circle for details.) Track and measure your results.

1. You gotta want it - Have the mindset that you are motivated to practice this for the sole purpose to improve. You have to be motivated to want to get better at this. You have to commit to practice it with the sole intention of improving your performance, not just go through it for fun. This mindset might seem trivial, but it is a huge factor in how your practice will pay off. Focus on the skill in front of you and remind yourself that how you are about to practice it will get you to your goal.

2. Analyze the skill to be practiced and break it down into small parts. Almost any skill you are working on can be broken down into smaller parts. Analyze your skill and see what the logical points to work on would be. How many parts should you have? It depends on the skill but 2 to 5 parts work great. Any more than that and I recommend you break the overall skill up into multiple sections, or into sets of smaller parts.

If you are working on your golf drive there are many components that go into that. You could break it down in a variety of ways. The mental process before you even step up to the ball, the grip, the setup, the beginning of your swing, the backswing, the forward swing, hip movement, the hit point, the follow through. You could certainly break it down more, but that would give you a few things to consider. You can see there are a lot of individual parts there to work on, so you may want to work on the mental pre routine, grip and setup as set one, then the actual movement as the second set.

If you are working on a piano piece a logical breakdown is looking at what the right hand is doing and then what the left hand is doing. You might find there are 3 different parts representing what the right hand is doing during the passage you are working on, so break those down as well.

If you are practicing your Spanish you might look at a sentence and go over the Nouns and Verbs, then consider the punctuation, or work on certain words by themselves. You may break it down more and take a 3 syllable word and work on each syllable separately.

Deciding how to break a skill down isn't an exact science so don't stress out over it. Just always try to find the smallest part that you can practice, then glue it back together with the other parts to form the whole.

3. Work on these parts individually using various techniques. Once you've analyzed the skill and identified the small parts, the next step is to work on those small parts individually with a variety of techniques. It often helps to practice the same part with several different SMART techniques, such as: *Right, Wrong, Right - Super Slo-Mo - Do it Different* etc.

Intense focus on each component of the skill will help super charge the whole thing once you put it all together.

4. Put the small parts together and work on the whole, again using various techniques. After you have worked on the individual parts and feel like they are solid, it's time to put them together and reassemble the complete skill. As you glue the parts back together, you will likely find that the transition between some parts may need some extra work. This is the time to identify those spots. Then work on those transitions by themselves, just going from Part A to Part B several times, for example, to make sure it is smooth.

With some skills, working on the individual components seems easier due to the fact that there are less moving parts and less things to think about. When you put the parts back together it can seem like a lot of information. That is why working as long as you need on the individual parts, until you get them into muscle memory for physical tasks, or get them committed to subconscious knowledge will help make the shift to putting all the parts together much more comfortable.

5. Analyze and track your effectiveness along the way. Get feedback from an instructor, or self analysis by using the *Four R Circle*. Track and measure your results. Along the path of mastering this skill, getting feedback from an instructor is immensely helpful. But whether or not you have access to an instructor, you should be continuously analyzing yourself by using the *Four R Circle* to help you assess and fine tune your skill. Always track, measure and review your progress in your practice notebook.

So whenever you sit down to start working on anything, put it through these 5 SMART steps and you will find that whatever you are doing will be more organized and clear for you to tackle. One other benefit of putting things through this regimen of steps is that it will help keep your mind from meandering and wondering what you should do next. It simply gives you a blueprint of what to do when you start to practice!

Part Four: Overcoming Obstacles

21: The Practice Minefield

Navigating the Practice Minefield. What is the practice minefield? This is a term I use to describe the myriad of things that can potentially derail your practice.

Distractions, frustration, lack of confidence, boredom, burnout, lack of time, procrastination, and fear of failure are just some of the traps we have to avoid as we try to get better at something. Keeping our practice on track is not just about what to do, it's also about what not to do, or what mines to avoid.

The practice minefield is something we all have to make our way through in order to have effective practice. We have to strategically weave our way through the field, avoiding the mines that are ready to explode and throw us off our game. Some of these rear their ugly heads just as we are hitting our stride and seeing real improvement. Some of them may come at us before we even start! Regardless, they are real and have to be dealt with.

Steven Pressfield talks about "The Resistance" in *The War of Art*, and reminds us that it is inevitable that we will face trials when we try to move forward. He says, "Any act that rejects immediate gratification in favor of long-term growth, will elicit resistance."[1] Practicing a skill is a long-term growth proposition for sure, so expect resistance.

How can we deal with all these things that are trying to thwart our progress? The first step is getting familiar with them so we'll recognize them when they start to happen. Then we can take steps to keep ourselves on track.

Let's look at some of the main obstacles you will need to overcome in order to keep your practice propelling you forward!

22: Distractions

Distractions can come at us from all directions. Sometimes they are sneaky and appear as an innocent little side project that needs our attention. Sometimes they are dressed up as an opportunity you just can't pass up. It doesn't matter what form they take, they need to be dealt with the same as any good intergalactic warrior would deal with a renegade shapeshifter: Exterminate.

One of the biggest problems with distractions is not just the time you are distracted, but the fact that it is difficult to get back on track and regain your focus.

Studies by Gloria Mark, associate professor at the Donald Bren School of Information and Computer Sciences at the University of California show that it can take 23 minutes to get back to your previous focus level once you have been distracted.[1]

23 minutes! That makes giving in to a distraction a costly proposition! You might be in a situation where you have a very limited time to practice in the first place, so you can't afford to take time off for distractions or you'll never get your practice in.

Some distractions are predictable and common, but some can seem to come at you from out of nowhere.

We sometimes hear the term SOS – or *Shiny Object Syndrome* to describe what happens when we jump from one thing to the next new thing. We are basically chasing the next shiny object we see, thereby taking our focus off what we should be doing and leaving the previous task incomplete.

This is a distraction in the world of practicing for sure. If you are working on your golf game; "I spent this week at practice trying out my new titanium super lightweight diamond putter." Yeah, but wasn't it just last week that you spent your practice time with that new carbon fiber super X never miss putter?

Lots of shiny objects.

It is just like the only too common tale of a guitarist buying and playing around with new effects, amps and any other gizmo that can make his guitar sound like a keyboard or a drum or a whatever, instead of simply spending his time practicing how to play the guitar.

The other distraction that can certainly be related to Shiny Object Syndrome is what I call MFDS. This is *Magic Fairy Dust Syndrome*.

Most of us who want to improve a skill would love to find a shortcut. If that comes in the form of a new putter or a new effects pedal, so be it. But whatever it is, for crying out loud get it here now! As long as we can just sprinkle some magic fairy dust on it and have our skill instantly improve, then it is all good.

Don't think the folks selling those putters and effects don't know that is how our minds work. "The world's most accurate putter" the ad says. Really? It just putts by itself? But often we want to believe in the shortcut so bad that we allow that distraction to pull us away from our mission.

I once had a guitar student illustrate this way of thinking

perfectly.

He had been struggling with getting his scales clean and as fast as he wanted. After he played them a few times he shook his head in frustration and said "I just can't get it". I told him not to worry because I was going to tell him exactly what he needed to master it and keep from being frustrated. He sat upright, with an excited look on his face and said "Really? What is it?" I just looked at him. The smile went away from his face and he said "Oh... practice?" with a little sarcasm around the edges of his crooked mouth.

I told him he was right, and then he uttered the line that perfectly captured this whole MFD syndrome. He said "Dang, I was hoping you were going to tell me it was something I could buy." He almost had his wallet out! He was so hopeful there was a shortcut. Even though the true way of just practicing was free, and much more gratifying, it didn't matter, because buying something would fix it NOW!

When I was a little kid I had a Snoopy poster that hung in my room. It was a picture of Snoopy standing on a step ladder looking over a fence. It said "The grass is always greener on the other side... until you get there and discover it's artificial turf!" That is what most of the Shiny Objects are, just things to fool you and take you off task.

Another distraction that can really mess us up is when we have several different skills we are working on at the same time. This one is especially deceptive because we legitimately want to improve multiple things, so it seems like it should be perfectly acceptable to just do them all at once! However, trying to jump back and forth between skills leads to problems.

"Multi-tasking" is the term we like to throw around. We think that we should be able to get more done by cramming more into the same time slot.

The problem? It doesn't work.

"Task-switching" is a better name for this as we really can't do multiple things at once, so we fool ourselves into thinking we can, by quickly bouncing back and forth between them. But studies at Stanford University by Clifford Nass and his colleagues showed that people who try to Multi-task or Task-switch; don't remember well, can't stay focused, are more easily distracted and are "suckers for irrelevancy."[2]

Yikes! Doesn't sound like trying to practice more than one skill at a time is a good idea.

Staying organized and focused on the practice at hand until you are finished with that is the key. Then you can stop practicing that skill, and begin something else. That allows you to devote your entire focus to what you are working on. If you are working on your piano skills, make sure you complete that before you start working on your Spanish. One skill focus at a time will make your practicing much more effective!

Most of us have multiple skills we would like to practice and improve. Multiple skill development just takes discipline and the ability to focus on what is at hand. A good practice system can help keep you on track. The SMART Zone Practice schedule will help you stay focused on what you specifically need to do.

Here's a *one, two punch* that will help you successfully deal with distractions.

1.   Accept that distractions will inevitably happen.
2.   Have a plan for how to react when they do.

My recipe for when I get distracted is this:

1. Stop.
2. Step back.
3. Re-focus.
4. Then think about what the very next step should be.

Don't think about anything else, just that next step that needs to happen to get back to moving forward. Put all of your focus on that!

If you can shake yourself away from the distraction and you have a method of getting back on track – then the distractions you will face simply become part of the overall process and just another thing you know how to deal with on your way to excelling at your skill! Always just do the *next thing*, that can pull you right back onto the path.

Some people make the mistake of thinking they can just wait for the distraction to end, and then they will get back on track. The error of this way of thinking is that often distractions beget distractions and before you know it you are in an avalanche of distractions and being swept down the hill away from your practicing! Don't wait for everything to get back to perfect after a distraction, just jump right back into it.

C.S. Lewis said it best: "If we let ourselves, we shall always be waiting for some distraction or other to end before we can really get down to our work. The only people who achieve much are those who want knowledge so badly that they seek it while the conditions are still unfavorable."

Remember, our minds are easily swayed and can often get distracted. It is a matter of keeping our mental focus sharp and staying the course of what we know we need to do.

Fight the urge to chase shiny new objects and fall for

sketchy shortcuts. Stick with your practice system. *Keep your focus on what you are practicing and constantly tackle the next thing.* That will result in the payoff you really want!

23: Frustration

Research tells us that frustration is one of the most common reasons given by people who quit something.

No real surprise there, right? I remember deciding to pursue riding a horse as a kid – until he bucked me off and I hit my head so hard on the ground I threw up! That led to frustration, which led to me quitting that pursuit!

So the good news is no, it's not just you! The bad news is that it's a very real problem and left unchecked can make you not only want to give up on what you are frustrated with, but can also lead to hesitation moving forward with other things for fear of getting to that same frustrated place. (You can only smack your head on the ground so many times before you get a little leery!)

It's no wonder we get frustrated with skills we are trying to improve. It is hard to stick with anything as is witnessed by the fact that 50% of us make New Year's resolutions, but only about 8% stick with them! Those are not good numbers, and I would imagine many of us who don't keep resolutions have bailed due to frustration.

How can we beat those odds and succeed at getting better?

If you are frustrated with how you are progressing with your practice (or not progressing as the case may be), there are a couple of things to consider.

First is whether or not you are practicing in the most effective way. In other words are you following a practice *system* with a clear list of objectives, a way to schedule your time, track your results and get feedback on your path? If not, it could be that you are just putting in time on the wrong things, just *playing* instead of *practicing*. So consider how you are actually spending your time and try to clarify these things by going over the steps in this book.

Second is something that often comes up, which is we all expect too much too soon. We get frustrated because we want the end result right now. When a student enters his first year of med school you don't hear him say "I am so frustrated, I want to do brain surgery now". He knows that it will take x amount of years before he can do that, so he just focuses on the work and tasks that are on the path before him. Eventually that will lead to where he wants to be. However, sometimes people practicing other disciplines have trouble seeing the progression of steps if they don't have an organized system of practice to help keep them on track. Remind yourself that you are on a journey, with ups and downs along the way.

When training Frisbee dogs, one of the most common mistakes I see people make is expecting too much too soon. They get a new dog out there and they wind up and chuck a Frisbee 40 yards and the dog just stands there puzzled and looks at them as if to say, "What? Am I supposed to go get that?"

When we start dogs out, it is a series of baby steps. First we get them interested in the disc as it is moved back and forth in front of them on the ground. Then we get them to tug with it, then chase it as it is rolled a short distance away from them. It isn't thrown yet, just rolled on the ground. Then the dog learns to take it out of your hand. Then it is let go of when they take it which will turn into tiny little 1 foot throws. Those throws get longer over time, but only slightly; 2 feet, 5 feet, 8 feet, 10 feet. Always making sure the dog is successful at each stage. If they are not, then you go back a stage and start again! This process can take weeks or months. It is very gradual with most dogs and you can't rush it!

So it is with skill acquisition for us humans as well. We need to start by just getting excited about it, and then taking baby steps gradually building up to what we want to accomplish.

"Everyone starts out bad, regardless of what they are practicing for. If you want to live a life that matters, don't start when you get good; start now so you become good." John Maxwell

I have been a professional guitarist most of my adult life. I have released 8 CDs, toured around the world, been written up in magazines etc. However, I have tapes from when I first picked up the guitar and tried to pluck a few notes. Holy smokes! It is awful! Out of tune, out of key, and certainly without a trace of rhythm. I wouldn't give the guy on those tapes any hope to be able to make music, let alone imagine he would ever be able to convince anyone to actually pay to listen to him! So what gives?

The point is, that anytime we are learning a new skill, we all start in the same place. Whatever the skill is you want to get better at, you are going to start by plucking out some bad notes! Don't let that frustrate you! This is a huge point of frustration for so many people who are trying to get better at something.

This even applies to someone who is already accomplished at something but has decided to get even better with practice. Where you are is where you are. So start right there! The key thing to remember is you are on the path to getting better, so don't worry about how good you are now. Think about how good you will be after a few months of practice!

Expect it to be bad before it gets good. We have heard the line "It's always darkest before the dawn," which is generally used to lift someone's spirits when they are going through a rough time. If you are frustrated with your practice, this applies as well.

Fight the SAG

We all get to a point in our practicing that I call the SAG. Yes your practice can start to sag just like that tired old shelf in your garage. The shelf sags because you have too many half full cans of old house paint stacked on it or perhaps it's piled too high with assorted things you should've thrown away years ago. Your practicing sags because it gets to that point where the excitement of the newness of working on something has worn off but you are not quite to the point where it's fun and exciting because you have gotten good! It is just tired and sagging.

But our SAG is also an acronym. It stands for *Slow Apathetic Grind!* Let's face it. Sometimes that is exactly what practicing can feel like - a grind.

The apathetic part is the feeling that you are not quite sure if what you are doing is going to work, and not sure if you are actually seeing any progress. Do you remember the movie *The*

Graduate? The Dustin Hoffman character decides he is going to marry the Katharine Ross character but unfortunately, she is in the process of getting married to someone else. Dustin breaks into the church mid-ceremony and whisks her off leaving her family and a jilted husband in shock. The two then hop on a bus, and in the closing scene they have the same looks on their faces as many of us get in the SAG stage of practice. They think this is going to work, but have a feeling of "now what," and a definite look of uncertainty and a little bit of questioning if they are doing the right thing. Well that's the feeling of the SAG! A lot of people quit at this point.

You have to fight it, breakthrough it and not get bogged down. Keep reminding yourself that practicing the right things in the right way will make you better in the long run even if you don't see it now. Later, we will look at some techniques that can help you fight the grind. But just know it is possible to get through it!

Frustrations are a natural part of any worthwhile endeavor. The key is how you deal with them. With a little thinking you will be able to conclude that the frustration you are experiencing is not a final roadblock, but rather just an obstacle that you can work your way around.

Steps to deal with frustrations:

1. Don't ignore your feelings of frustration. Instead, when you feel this way, stop and acknowledge it. This can not only help you find a way to get through it, but it also gives you the power that comes from realizing that it is only a temporary state.

2. Look at the specific areas or things that can be directly

causing your frustration. Sometimes it can be as simple as a new way to attack a certain area of your skill that can fix everything. Dig in and find the solution!

3. Get excited! Why? Because if you are frustrated you are usually just about to have a breakthrough! Frustrations usually come as you are reaching a tough point. Once you get through, it will lead you to a better place.

When you get frustrated, that is a good time to step back and regroup. Look at your practice system and see if it needs tweaking. Make any adjustments and then dig in.

24: Procrastination

"The trouble with most people is that they quit before they start." Thomas Edison

Often the biggest obstacle to getting better is just getting started!

By reading this you have taken a step in getting past procrastination. However, it can still jump in your path at any time and obstruct your improvement. Every time you decide to work on your SMART practice plan you have to deal with it, each time you schedule a practice session you have to push it aside.

Again, Steven Pressfield cautions we can get fooled into thinking we are not avoiding practice, but we are just postponing it. "Procrastination is the most common manifestation of Resistance because it's the easiest to rationalize. We don't tell ourselves, 'I'm never going to write my symphony.' Instead we say, 'I am going to write my symphony; I'm just going to start tomorrow.'"[1]

That is of course true with starting anything, a diet, exercise program, a practice plan, or quitting a bad habit. This thinking even affects our favorite heroine in *Gone with the Wind*, where Scarlett O'Hara says on multiple occasions, "I'll think about it tomorrow."

But what is procrastination and why do we do it? The basic premise of procrastinating or putting things off comes down to your view of the value of doing the thing now versus doing something else now. If something else seems to have more value in any way (even if it is just more pleasure from doing something that is more fun), then it makes it easy to put off what you were going to do until later.

With practice, as we have talked about, there is often a limited amount of time to do it, so any delay is not going to be good. Practice that you will "do tomorrow," is just practice that you didn't do today, and will not move your development forward.

Legendary golfer, Ben Hogan, who was one of the pioneers of taking practice seriously in order to improve his game, sums it up simply and brilliantly. "Every day you miss practicing is one day longer it takes to be good."

Here are a few tips to keep you from stepping on the procrastination mine.

1. Of course the best thing you can do is to have a complete practice plan, and review it. When you feel like putting off your practice, just review your goals, Skillbox Inventory lists, and use that to get you going.

2. Tell yourself you will just practice for a short time. Once you just get started, that usually inspires you to keep going longer.

3. If you are practicing something that you usually do by yourself, try doing it with a friend. Looking forward to

getting together with someone can fire you up.

4. Make sure your goal has a timeline - and review it, or set a deadline for it. That can give you a sense of urgency and jump you back on track.

5. If you find yourself constantly putting off practice, you might want to re-clarify what you are trying to do. Maybe you have lost interest in this pursuit, or maybe you just need to get a new sense of why you are doing it.

Procrastinating is another normal thing you will experience from time to time as you practice getting better at something. Just realize that it doesn't have to completely derail you.

25: Find Your Johnson

If you want to find motivation to practice, you need to find your Johnson. Well, more precisely you need to find your Kent Johnson. When I was a teenager and learning to play guitar, my instructor Steve understood what motivated me. He knew I was pretty competitive and could stand to be pushed a bit. So he did.

I have to admit, although I worked really hard at guitar, I was also a semi-rebellious teenager and could be a slacker at times, especially when sitting at home alone practicing scales was juxtaposed with hanging out in town with various members of the opposite sex. Working towards long term achievement can often become obfuscated by the allure of instant gratification, for teenagers as well as adults!

In our small town I was the only person I knew who was studying guitar. I had to drive 20 miles to the neighboring town to take guitar lessons, or find anyone else who was learning to play.

One of the other students who was taking lessons from my guitar instructor was a kid named Kent Johnson. I only knew Kent casually, through a mutual friend, but I knew he had started playing guitar about the same time I had, and was roughly the same age.

My instructor would occasionally mention Kent as being one of his star students, just in passing to let me know he was studying from the same books and material I was. I hated reading music, and consequently, that was the worst part of my guitar playing. My instructor seemed to take special pleasure in making me learn how to read, so I slogged through the Berklee series of books. My "I left my book at home," tactic to try and get out of reading at lessons only worked a couple of times until he started making sure he had a copy of the book I was working on with him whenever I came in for my lesson. When I would be whining about having to work on reading instead of learning a Van Halen solo, he would just casually say, "OK... but Kent Johnson is already in book 2." That would usually make me cave in and do the reading work.

In my mind Kent occupied the role of antagonist. He always seemed to be one step ahead of me. Once again, I didn't really know him, and for all I knew he might not have even still been playing guitar. He could have moved on to playing the tuba, but the thought of him pushed me to practice just so I wouldn't have to listen to my instructor tell me how good he was.

The absolute pinnacle of my instructor's drive to keep me on the practice track came by way of a couple of messages left on my home answering machine. I was, of course, still living with my parents at that time, so it was technically the family answering machine.

The first of the messages I remember, came on a Saturday night. I had been out late and came home to a message on the machine. It was from my instructor. It was short, and simply went like this: "Jeff, are you practicing tonight? - because Kent Johnson is." Click. Brilliant! Now of course I am pretty sure he didn't know if Kent was indeed practicing that night or not, but it was just a subtle little jab to make me consider what I was doing with my time.

It worked pretty well. Thanks Steve!

I remember several years later as I was on the road with a band and there was a party after the gig. I had considered going with the rest of the band to the party, but then I had a thought. "I wonder if Kent is at a party tonight, or if he is home practicing?" I stayed in the hotel to practice. I would occasionally think of that when I knew I needed to practice. I had not heard about Kent in years, but that didn't matter. He had become a composite of all things that drove me to practice.

I have used this method of identifying my motivations to drive me to become better at anything I need to practice.

Most people who have succeeded in anything in life, whether it be art, sports, or business, can usually point to something that motivated them. Often it is a nemesis, or an archenemy who drives them to achieve. Sometimes it is something that inspires them and is uplifting. It can be a person, either an opponent you are competing against, or someone who inspires you. It can be a circumstance that pushes or pulls you. Maybe you want to get away from your past, or maybe you want to arrive at a specific version of the future that suits you. But there is usually something.

Superman had Lex Luthor to keep him motivated to fight evil. I would imagine Steve Jobs and Bill Gates used the thought of each other to stay up late and work extra hard.

In Tokyo, on a magical night in 1990, James "Buster" Douglas shocked the world when he knocked out the previously unbeatable "Iron" Mike Tyson, to become the Heavyweight Champion of the world. So how did the 40 to 1 underdog do it? Three weeks before the fight, Buster's mother had passed away suddenly from a heart attack. According to Buster, thinking about his mother drove him to win. He had something.

The next time you think about practicing, start out by spending a little time considering what it is that drives you to get better at this. Really think about it. Let it motivate you. Let it stir your soul.

Find your Johnson.

26: Time Enough

"I just don't have enough time to practice." This could be the most popular excuse for not getting better at something. It's not without merit. There are only 24 hours in a day, and necessity dictates we fill them up with things like work, sleep and eating. That, along with a healthy dose of family time, endless home projects, social time with friends, and most likely more hours than could possibly be necessary, checking email and surfing online, leaves us with very little precious time to practice. That is especially true if you have more than one thing you are trying to get better at.

Composer Leonard Bernstein said, "To achieve great things, two things are needed; a plan, and not quite enough time." Mr. Bernstein is alluding to the fact that when we don't have quite enough time, we will push ourselves and get focused on getting it done.

If we just look at the part about not having enough time, if that's the case I am on to great things for sure! Because I NEVER seem to have enough time! Do you ever feel that way? Like if you only had a little more time, you'd get to all those things you want to get better at. But would you?

I have found that many times the issue of "not having enough time to practice," stems from two things. *Basic time management,* and the *inability to prioritize.*

Time has a sneaky way of slipping away from us. Most of us realize that time is a valuable commodity in life, and we really want to make the best use of it. Actually putting that into practice is the tricky part. We have the best intentions of making the most of our time, but often end up feeling like Louis Boone who said, "I am definitely going to take a course on time management, just as soon as I can work it into my schedule."

Sometimes we describe a vast undertaking by saying, "You could write a book on it!" Well in the case of time management, it's not just that you could write a book on it, it's that there are already hundreds of books written on the subject. This shows not only our interest in it, but also our inability to master it.

For our purposes of making sure we have time to get our practice sessions in, let's look at a couple of time management principles we can use immediately.

The first principle that is essential to getting your practice time in, is to schedule your practice time the same as you would a doctor's appointment, an important meeting at work, or a hot date! Put it in your daily or weekly schedule, and stick to it.

Get in the habit of scheduling your practice right alongside your other important events. Planning or scheduling your time is probably something that you are currently doing for other things in your life, but sometimes we treat things like practice as "extras" or things we will do "when we have time." Of course this usually leads to not getting to your practice time at all.

The great news is that once you schedule a block of time to practice, you will then be able to use the SMART Zone practice plan to map out exactly what to work on in the time you have allotted, making whatever practice time you have effective and efficient!

What we are talking about is treating practice time with a little more importance. Elevate it to something you schedule and commit to.

The second principle is making practice time a priority. Often we have something we want to get better at, but because we don't make it a priority in our lives it gets squashed by all the other things clamoring for our time and attention. Then it comes time to perform, and the realization that we haven't made practice a priority becomes painfully clear.

I remember years ago seeing a friend come to this realization right before my eyes sitting in a small cafe in the jungle in Mexico. We had just been on a long hike and were more than a little thirsty and hungry. We found this little cafe where the ratio of dogs to humans sitting on the patio seemed about equal.

A little background on my friend. He had decided to learn to speak Spanish about a year before this trip. "I'm gonna do it," was his boast as I recall. But, since he didn't really make it a priority, he never seemed to have time to practice. A few months before the trip I asked him how his Spanish was going, to which he replied, "Yeah, I really gotta start practicing more." Bad sign.

As we sat in the cafe surrounded by the beautiful sounds of jungle birds with sun rays streaming onto the terrace, I had to witness my friend desperately try to find the right words to order his lunch. He was determined to order in Spanish, but he wasn't quite there yet and had to keep opening his translation book and sounding out words as the waiter stood patiently with pen in hand and a puzzled look on his face.

In between his thumbing through the pages of his *Spanish Words You Must Know* book, I was able to order my lunch using plain old English and pointing to a few things in the menu, then nodding affirmatively when the waiter would say a word I recognized.

Eventually my friend said, "I'll have what he's having" and stuck his book back in his bag slightly disgusted. I didn't have to say anything to elicit a frustrated explanation from him. He of course knew my views on practice and getting better, so felt the need to give his story. "I know," he started, "I had really wanted to be able to come down here and at least have 'some' fluency. But with the kids getting out of school, and my wife starting her new job... well, I guess I just didn't make it a priority."

No real harm done in this case. The food was excellent as was the setting. However, this just illustrates what happens to anything we want to get better at but don't make a priority. In this case it only impacted my friend's pride, but it can be something that keeps us from achieving many things.

If you want to practice something, you need to make it a priority to do so or it will just end up another thing you "didn't have time for."

Here are a few ways to reinforce practice as a priority:

1. Don't think of the practice, think of *what you are practicing for*. It might be hard to see getting up at 5am and running 5 miles before you go to work as an exciting thing you want to make a priority. But, if that will lead to finally being able to compete in a marathon, then that is an exciting thing! So look at the big picture of what practice is going to do for you, and where it

will take you.

2. If you have decided to get better at something, have taken the steps to map out your goals and look at your Skillbox inventory, you have already committed to this. Look at the time you have spent doing that and it will help you see this is indeed important to you, so make the time for practicing it a priority.

3. Consider what will happen if you *don't* practice this. Sometimes considering the consequences of not practicing will inspire you to make practice a priority.

When it comes to the importance of your practice time, guard it like a treasure, and remember what Johann Wolfgang Von Goethe said: "Things which matter most must never be at the mercy of things which matter least."

Part Five: Tools, Tips and Techniques

27: **Practice Notebook**

"The distance from the attachment of one ear to the other is equal to that from the meeting of the eyebrows to the chin, and in a fine face the width of the mouth is equal to the length from the parting of the lips to the bottom of the chin."

So reads an entry from one of Leonardo Da Vinci's notebooks in a chapter called "On the Proportions and on the Movements of the Human Figure."

Thomas Edison amassed over 5 million pages of notes and documents written by himself and his team about their processes and experiments.

Yet the excuse I hear most often from people who don't keep a practice notebook is, "I just don't have time to write things down in a practice notebook."

Da Vinci and Edison are not just average run of the mill humans. They are two of the most productive humans in history, and if they saw it wise to take time away from the actual work of the task at hand to write detailed notes, then we should consider following their lead. It is true they were not writing information about practicing, but rather about their inventions. However, by writing in your practice notebook you are taking steps to *invent* a new level of skill for yourself!

History is replete with high achievers who have kept

exquisite notebooks and journals. It seems to go hand in hand with their success.

In our SMART Practice Notebook, we should keep all of the details regarding our practice system. This should include written versions of our goals, our 3 Skillbox Inventory lists, and our SMART Zone Schedule. We also want to have a section to keep notes on each practice session.

The best way I've found to trigger immediate improvement in the effectiveness of your practicing is to get into the habit of logging notes about your practice sessions.

But taking the *right* kind of notes is the key. Here's how to do that.

It is important to be able to capture both quantitative and qualitative information about your practice. Quantitative data deals with anything that can be measured, such as number of sets or reps you do something. It doesn't address how well it was done or deal with the *quality* of how you did it. That is where the qualitative data comes in.

Let's look at an example of using both quantitative and qualitative information to track a practice session of working on free throws on the basketball court. You may start out with writing down the quantitative or numbers portion of your notes:

Made 15 out of 25 the first set – Made 21 out of 25 the second set.

While that gives you some good data, it doesn't tell the whole story. You need the qualitative information to help you understand why the second set was better. Such as:

In the second set I told myself to relax and keep my arm speed slower. I was rushing in the first set but for the second set I slowed down and took a deeper breath before each shot.

Something as simple as this information can give you awesome clues as you look back on your sessions to determine what worked and what didn't. Seeing what caused the improvement in your better second round might trigger you to later add "relax" to the list of little things that make a huge difference!

Revisit that issue of not having enough time to write down practice notes.

The thing that is important to recognize, is with a practice *system* – writing down notes and tracking your results IS a part of practicing. This is one of the mind shifts that has to take place as we get serious about improving. Understanding that a complete practice system includes not only the actual physical practicing but also the preparation and planning, along with the tracking, note taking, analyzing and assessing.

"You have to look at yourself objectively. Analyze yourself like an instrument. You have to be absolutely frank with yourself." Audrey Hepburn

Your practice notebook/journal can be old school analog or geeked out digital. It can be as elaborate as a computer or tablet, as easy to access as your phone, or as simple as a paper notebook and pen. You can even jot down notes on the back of a napkin or piece of scrap paper and transfer them into an organized system later. The important thing is to get used to doing it on a regular basis.

Find the method that works best for you and stick with it! If you dig entering data in a spreadsheet and looking at various numbers – then do that. If you hate looking at a spreadsheet and just want to have a short sentence or two about your session, do that. Doing what you like will make you stick with it, and that is the key.

Your notes can be as in depth as you like, and more information is always good. However, if time is an issue you can do the minimum, just so you have a reference to look back on.

Almost all of us have our phones with us wherever we go. This wonderful little device can be completely annoying, but it can also be an awesome practice tool when used as a video camera, audio recorder, notebook, and general storage unit for anything you want to record about your practice time.

How I Use My Phone For Practice Notes

For example I use my phone to do some very basic short notes when I am out practicing throwing Frisbee's for disc dogging. I make simple notes of the wind – and what worked. This isn't an exact science, but gives me some point of reference on the fly. I use a program called Evernote for keeping track of my practice notes. I just open the app, draw a rectangle, add a couple of arrows about wind direction then a line or two of notes on what worked and what didn't. It takes me about 2 minutes.

SMART Practice

Moderate steady wind - some gusts across

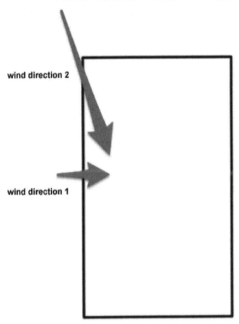

Throwing from this side not as good, although it can work - no hyzer, maybe annhyzer, spin and nose up just a hair and a little higher

wind direction 2

wind direction 1

Throwing from this side is best. With hyzer, snap, normal height. Can hyzer in from the right side. Don't let it flip or it will float wide right.

The thing about most of the information on these notes, is it is stuff I already know. Like I already know that I like to throw into a slight left to right headwind. So why the heck do I write this down? Well, for one it solidifies and confirms it, and as I add this one note to many others it serves to create a big picture of all the variables.

Also at events when I am getting ready to hit the field and throw into this same wind, I can look at a graphic that tells me – Yeah, I throw GREAT in this wind, whooohoooo! That can give me confidence and take some of the over-thinking out of my game. Keeping these notes on your practice will pay off in many ways!

Mining the Nuggets!

One thing I highly suggest you do is regularly review your practice notes and make a separate list of important points. This will then help you come up with a *quick check list* of maybe the top 7 things to pay special attention to. Then review that each time before you compete or perform.

You are basically *mining* the crucial nuggets of helpful tips and information from your practice time which will allow you to create an overview of what you should be focusing on when it is time to perform.

Another great benefit of this, is that instead of feeling like your practice sessions are just one time events that you are beseeching a higher power to magically use to build your skill over time – when you pull tips from each session it makes that session continue to shape what you do in a more tangible way. Making this list of highlights of your practice time is a powerful habit!

Journaling and assessing your practice time is one of the things that can give you an edge on the competition. Why? Because many of them do not take notes, keep accurate records, or assess their practice. Without a doubt, reviewing what you have done, what has worked and what has not worked, gives you the best insight into what you need to do next!

Whether someone is working on shaving a couple strokes off of their casual golf game, or working on a world changing idea like Thomas Edison, tracking your progress is essential.

The habit of writing down some practice notes will give you a more clear understanding of how you are doing and what you should be working on to get to the next level.

Ben Franklin was another productive individual. He was well known for his detailed note keeping. His *13 virtues* were character traits he endeavored to cultivate within himself. He tracked his progress on each virtue in a notebook that also kept morning and evening thoughts that he would write down about his accomplishments.

How important did he feel this tracking and writing down his progress was? At the end of his life he said, "I am indebted to my notebook for the happiness of my whole life."

So if you are not taking notes on your practice sessions, start doing it today! If you already have a practice notebook, review it and make sure it contains everything you need to make your practice successful. Remember to log both quantitative and qualitative information for the complete picture. That will give you some of Ben's happiness when you see your skill improving!

28: Make it Easy

One thing is certain. You are more likely to stick with a practice plan if it is easy to practice. Not that the practice itself is easy, but getting to the point of actually being able to practice should be free from obstacles. How can you make it easy to get to that point?

You want to make it not only easy, but productive, comfortable and inspiring to practice. How you do that will depend on what skill you are going to practice, and where you do it. Do you practice on a field? In a room? In a different place each time? Do you need some gear or equipment to practice?

We have spent a good deal of time discussing organizing your goals, skills, time and technique. The other thing we want to look at organizing and maximizing is your practice environment. A little thinking ahead of time can help get you into the flow of practice more effectively.

I know it's sometimes hard due to space limitations to have a *practice area* set up all the time. However, the rewards of doing this are huge! Try to organize your practice space if possible, and for sure organize your practice materials. The key is to be able to spend minimum time getting ready, and maximum time actually practicing!

Convenience and preparation

I remember living in a small apartment where due to space limitations I used to put my guitar in it's case after practice and slide it under the bed. I found myself not practicing as much as I wanted and the fix was simply to leave the guitar setting out on it's stand next to the chair I practiced in.

While having to drag it out of it's case from under the bed doesn't seem like a big deal, I can tell you that late at night after a long day when faced with digging out the guitar and cables and setting it all up vs. just crashing on the couch caused strain in my practice mettle! But when the guitar was sitting right there looking at me, it was easy to pick it up for just a few minutes, which would usually turn into a few hours. "Out of sight, out of mind" can apply here.

Many successful diet plans are based on organizing and even preparing your meals ahead of time. The idea is if you have to go to the work of collecting ingredients and cooking something up when you finally realize you are hungry, you will most likely not take the time to "do it right." However, if you prepare healthy meals ahead of time, then it is easy to just go to the freezer at lunch time and get out "Wednesday's lunch," eat it and be on your way.

Want to increase the odds you will go to the gym in the morning for a workout? Pack your gym bag the night before and set it on the table next to your car keys.

It's all about creating the least amount of friction between you and your practice. Having your practice materials organized not only makes it convenient, but can help take any mental stress out of the decision process to commit to practicing. Assorted genius' throughout history including the likes of Albert Einstein have been said to own several of the exact same sets of clothing so they don't waste any decision making energy on deciding what to wear each day when they open their closets.

If you think too much about whether you should practice, you will certainly come up with a lawn that needs to be mowed, a deck that needs to be stained, an email that should be sent, or just a couch that needs to be held down. There are many things that can pull your mind away from practice. Having things prepared ahead of time and convenient is one way to move the chances of completing your practice session in your favor.

Space Routine

I really like the idea of creating a practice area that is consistent and at least partially exclusive to practice. Many sleep studies have shown that not only doing a routine before bedtime but also treating your bedroom as a specific place to go for sleep will help you achieve a restful night. If your mind views your bedroom as a place to go watch TV, read a book for hours or just hang out, then it diminishes the potency of sleeping there. The same can work for your practice space.

I recall while studying Tae Kwon Do that we would get to the Dojang, go into the small dressing room and put on our uniform or *gi* and then step out onto the main floor mat. We would bow to our instructor and then get down to training. I remember that routine and space so well that even just thinking through it now makes me want to start kicking something! Having a set pattern to entering the practice zone is very helpful to get a jump start on your practice session.

If you can develop some consistency to your practice area and time, it can help you focus better, more quickly, and get into your practice groove.

Time

Just like going into a specific place can help you lock your focus on practicing, so can having a specific time. While it may not always be possible to practice at the same time, working on a schedule can have some positive benefits.

I accidentally developed a *prime time* for personal super creativity. This happened while I was touring as a professional guitarist. My band was playing almost every night of the week for several years. That meant from roughly 9:00 pm until 1:00 am I was playing guitar. I was creating solos and improvising parts. My creative thinking brain was turned *on* during this time on a regular basis.

When I got off the road, what time of the day do you think was the most creative for me? Absolutely! Late at night it was like a switch would click on and I would just feel more creative. I had better ideas, I could get into flow, and had great creative energy. This really helped me with practicing the guitar as well as coming up with creative solutions to anything else I was working on.

While I didn't set out to build a specific creative time, it became that simply due to repetition.

Various studies on writing have shown that if would be authors developed a specific time to sit down and write, they could start to be more prolific during that time.

Having a specific practice time will program your body and mind to achieve the most effective results during that time.

Practice Environment

There are many variables when you think about your normal practice space. What is the temperature? How is the lighting? What about sounds? An important thing to remember is that you have to assess what makes practice effective for you.

Some considerations for your practice space:

Color and lighting

Do we need to call in an interior decorator? Well, maybe not, however studies show that lighting and room color can greatly affect your emotions and thought process. It makes sense then to consider room color or the kind of lighting as possible elements in practice productivity.

Color Psychology basically looks at how we react to certain colors. While the complexity of various studies go beyond what we really need to discuss here, suffice it to say what color you surround yourself with can have a definite impact on your mood and performance. So consider the color of your practice area.

In general, Red is associated with desire and passion, it can raise your heart rate. Blue is said to help with focus and can create a calming effect. Yellow tends to be connected with creativity. While each color can affect you, which will be best for you depends on several things such as what exactly you are practicing (do you need to be calm, or fired up?) along with your personal reaction to color. So experiment! When we are talking about dialing in the best scenario to help us be successful practicers, we want to look at anything that may give us an edge!

Lighting also falls into a similar category as color as it can change your frame of mind as well. *A study in the Journal of*

Consumer Psychology showed that according to the researchers, brighter lights can amp up both positive and negative emotions. So the opposite is also true; "Turning down the light, effortless and unassuming as it may seem, can reduce emotionality in everyday decisions."[1]

Other studies have shown that people who spent afternoons in natural light were much more alert in the evening than those who spent their day in artificial light.

Just like color, what kind of lighting you apply to your practice area can depend on what your needs are for what you are about to practice. Consider whether your practice is intense and energetic, or thoughtful and measured.

Temperature

Anyone who has spent time in extreme cold or heat can certainly understand the concept of how temperature can get your attention. I recall sitting and freezing waiting for a tow truck to come and pull me out of a snowbank in rural Iowa where I grew up. I just remember that all I could think of was the cold and how I felt right then. I tried to "think warm thoughts," but it was impossible to get my focus on anything other than my chattering teeth!

Can slightly less extreme temperature changes make a difference in how we think, focus and perform? Absolutely say researchers in a study called *Effects of Body Temperature on Reasoning, Memory and Mood.* They say, "The increase in core temperature was associated with a significant increase in the speed of performance of the tests, by 11 and 10%, respectively. The warm immersions also induced a significant decrease in alertness."[2]

While it may be hard to dissect these studies in order to

come to a conclusive opinion on how to use temperature to make your practice more effective, it is safe to say that the temperature can certainly change your emotional and mental state. This just gives us one more variable to consider.

Once again, depending on what you are practicing you may find that a certain temperature works better for you. You need to experiment!

Sounds

Our last environmental factor we are going to briefly discuss is sound. What does it sound like where you practice? What are the natural sounds and what are the sounds you create?

When we think about practicing things like sports, we are often led to believe that listening to music will help. But will it? Well, it depends. Many studies have shown that listening to certain upbeat music can "pump you up." So if that is a state that practicing your particular skill benefits from, then some thumpin' and bumpin' might work for you. Of course there are also studies that show more soothing music can help your mind focus on specific tasks. Therefore if your practice requires a little mellower concentration, you might be helped by some elevator music!

Some people report that they practice best when their practice environment is completely free of noise of any kind. That allows them to put their entire focus on the task at hand.

What about natural sounds? If you have to practice at a location that has background noise that you can't directly control, you need to assess if it is distracting to your practice time. If so, noise cancelling headphones may help. Or adding noise such as music that you can control may help create the soundscape you need.

You have to decide if music, no music, background noise, or silence is the auditory element that will create the best practice space for you.

When we discuss all of these variables in your practice environment, the thing to keep in mind is this: You may be affected by one, all, or none of them in your practice area. However, you need to be aware that these could potentially make a difference. Especially when we start to *stack* the effects of multiple elements. A certain room color, paired with the right lighting, the perfect temperature with the right sound. Any one of these things may make a difference, but all together if you find the perfect combination it could really impact how effective your practice is.

To stay motivated to practice you want to remove any barriers and create an environment that is conducive to effective practice. Whether it is having your guitar sitting on the ready, having your gym bag pre-packed and in your car, or having your golf clubs, practice notebook and car keys all laying on the table ready to go when you get home from work, make it easy to practice.

Consider all the elements that make up your practice space, such as color, lighting, temperature and sounds. Having the right combination can kick your practice up to the next level.

29: Instructors and Coaches

Michael Jordan helped his team win the NBA championship 6 times. All 6 of those times he was voted the Finals MVP. He was an overall NBA MVP 5 times and an All Star 14 times. He is considered by many to be the greatest basketball player of all time. And yet, what did he tell Spike Lee was his most important asset? "My coach is everything," Jordan said in an interview with Spike.

If even a player of Jordan's stature not only uses a coach, but thinks they're "everything," then it is a pretty safe bet to assume we could all use one.

Having a coach, teacher, instructor or mentor can be the secret ingredient that ignites your practice and puts your skill over the top.

A good instructor can watch what you are doing and provide you with feedback and assessment of your technique. Often they can point out issues or problems you can't see yourself. Since they have likely been down the road you are on, and certainly worked with others in the same place, they can also help with guidance on the important question of *what to work on next.*

I have seen many students who have struggled for years to improve in a meaningful way start working with a good instructor and immediately see results. Students sometimes get "stuck in a rut" and just keep spinning their wheels, eventually getting frustrated. The right teacher can give you a clear way out of that rut.

But it has to be the *right* instructor. How do you find that right instructor?

In the old days the only option was to call the local music store, or the country club, or talk to the local college. You would basically book some time with the guitar teacher or tennis pro or tutor they set you up with, and hope for the best. This didn't always turn out optimal for the student. When the heavy metal guitar student gets sent to study with the elderly classical lady…. it is not the most favorable pairing!

However, today word of mouth about instructors for anything imaginable can be found in online recommendations, forums and various other social media outlets. Of course, most instructors have an online presence where you can go check out what they do. There are various sites that can connect an aspiring student with a coach or instructor for almost any skill you can imagine.

You may be able to find the instructor you are looking for in your local area, but if not, no problem. The options for studying online continue to expand and get better.

Often the student and instructor can communicate via email, phone or Skype. They can also simply exchange videos. The student can get feedback and guidance regardless of where the student and instructor live in the world. So there really is no excuse to not at least do some study with an instructor whether in your hometown or online.

Need help in figuring out what to look for in an instructor?

All of the organizing you have been doing with regards to your SMART Practice system will help here. Take a look at your goals, and where you currently are. Then make a list of the things you need help with. It may be as simple as help with a technique you are currently working on, or more complex guidance understanding what you need to work on next.

Once you have this list, then when you talk to different instructors you can be specific about what you need. Always tell them your ultimate goal. Let them know exactly what you hope to get out of lessons or coaching with them.

I always like to ask students to tell me what they hope to achieve in 3 months, 6 months and a year. That way I can chart out a path to take them where they want to go. Sometimes they are not realistic about what they can accomplish in a certain amount of time, so that is my job to keep them on track with both their expectations and their specific practice.

Once you have found the right instructor, your job as student is easy right? Just wait until they tell you what to do, then do it, and repeat. Wrong! This is the most certain way to end up frustrated.

The absolute key as a student is to communicate freely and often with your instructor! I can't emphasize this enough. I can't tell you how many students from various skills have told me they quit studying with their instructor because it just wasn't working. They often say "He didn't really help me with what I needed." Of course when I ask if they expressed this to their instructor, they said they hadn't. When I asked if they gave the instructor a detailed list of what they wanted to do now, and in the future, they said no.

Remember this: Instructors, coaches, and teachers are NOT mind readers. If you don't express to them what you want, how it is going, and if it is working or not, they can't adjust what they are teaching you or help you get on track. Just as important as working on the assignments your instructor gives you is the communication you have with your instructor. All good instructors rely on feedback from students to help with the next steps. Much of this feedback and assessment the instructor can decipher on their own, as they have the ability to see what is going on. However, student feedback can be enormously helpful in keeping it all running smooth!

As an instructor, my favorite students are the ones who ask questions constantly, and then apply my answers. It shows they are engaged in the whole process and want to learn and improve. It helps me guide them and get a feel for what may be tripping them up or what issues we need to address.

To recap what we have gone over.

1. A good instructor or coach is invaluable.

2. You can find one locally or online.

3. Create a list of what you want to do and what you already know and share that with any potential instructor.

4. Once you find your instructor, communicate often! Don't hesitate to tell them what is working and what isn't. Ask questions!

5. Remember, just having an instructor won't make you

better. Working with an instructor is an interactive relationship. Tell them what you want, do what they suggest, give them feedback on how it's working, and then trust the next steps they ask you to take.

30: Four R Circle

Did you ever get a rock tumbler for Christmas? I did when I was about ten years old. I remember being excited when I pulled that package out from under the tree.

A rock tumbler, or rock polisher, is basically a machine that creates smooth polished rocks out of ordinary rocks you find in your yard. It consists of a cylinder about the size of a half gallon of milk that you put the rocks in, which is attached to a motor that causes it to spin continuously.

I recall the instructions said to find some rocks that "had the potential to turn into amazing jewels." Well, I'm not sure how much potential there was in the first batch of rocks I picked up at the creek, but they were the best I could find at the time, and I was anxious to see this thing work it's magic!

I put the rocks in, then some solution to add the friction needed to impact the rocks, then turned it on. As you can imagine it made a horrendously loud sound as the rocks banged around and around in the cylinder. After an enthusiastic start it was pointed out that it may be a bit much to have this thing clanking away 24/7 on the dining room table, so my mom negotiated with us to move it out to the back porch, where it was only slightly less annoying.

After one full day of constant tumbling we shut it off, and

with a little trepidation we opened the lid to have a look inside. I wasn't expecting much, but to my surprise I could see the rocks already starting to get some of the rough edges knocked off of them. This might actually work! We started it back up and let it go for a few more days. Unaware of what was going on in there and having to wait to see, was much like a kid not knowing when the cookies were coming out of the oven. It was actually worse because instead of a 15 minute wait for cookies, this went on for days. With a few stops along the way the total process took a couple of weeks.

Once we shut it off after the final round and took those rocks out, they were smooth and shiny. I have to admit that my sense of wonder and my general trusting nature took a bit of a hit when we opened up the tumbler and these rocks looked just like the ones you could buy in a store. I figured those super shiny gems I had seen in stores were special stones that had come from some mystic secret place that resembled Tolkien's *Rivendell*. So to now run right smack into the reality that they could have just been pummeled smooth on someone's back porch was sort of a bummer for a 10 year old dreamer.

What I did learn about polishing rocks, was that it took time, patience, and a lot of work. You had to keep stopping and checking the rocks and then add more stuff in there to help smooth them out.

I have since come to realize that this is a great analogy for how we get better at things.

As you are practicing your skill, it is not only helpful, but necessary to track what you are doing and evaluate what is working and what you need to change. If you can work with an instructor to help analyze your practice and offer guidance along the way that is a great option. However, that may not be possible for you for a variety of reasons; cost, proximity to instructors, their availability and so on.

The next best thing to having an expert assess, evaluate, and give you feedback, is to do it yourself. It is important that SOMEONE is evaluating, so if you can't get ongoing access to an expert, you have to step outside yourself and analyze your own skill. You should get in the habit of doing this anyway, even if in conjunction with working with an instructor. This should just be a part of your overall practice system.

The best way to do this is with what I call the *Four R Circle*. This could really be called a *Skill Tumbler*. These four things do to your skill what my old rock tumbler did to those rocks. Any skill you put in will get run through the process and come out beautiful!

First let's list the four Rs, and then see how they work.

Record
Review
Refine
Repeat

That is the formula. If you apply this to any skill you are working on, or even any part of any skill, you will see improvement. It works every time!

Record

This first step of the process has become so much easier with advances in technology. Almost all of us have an extremely high quality device capable of recording audio, text and hd video that we carry with us at all times right in our pocket: Our phone.

While you can get elaborate setups to record yourself, it really isn't necessary, and I find that I am way more likely to use what is convenient.

How you record yourself performing your skill depends on the skill. If you are doing anything that requires physical movement, you definitely should use video. If however you are working on something that is more mental than physical, you may find that just writing your thoughts down works. Just make sure you "record" your effort in a way that will allow you to do the next "R."

Review

Now that you have recorded yourself performing your skill, or the part of your skill you are working on, the next step is to review it. This is hard for some of us. Particularly anyone who is overly critical of themselves in the first place. A singer may not be able to stand hearing their own voice. A person working on public speaking may think they look silly onstage. A golfer may be too distracted by the "extra pounds" the camera adds to their body to analyze their swing. Many people have a difficult time self analyzing without being overly self critical.

The key is this: You have to take off the student's hat and put on the instructor's hat. You have to develop the ability to look at your performance of the skill just like you would look at a student you were trying to help. You wouldn't say, "That's terrible, you are awful" to someone you were coaching would you? Of course not. You might say, "That is a great start. Let's look at some spots we can make even better." The problems you see are the same, and the issues you need to work on are identical. What is different is how you approach it. Many of us don't give ourselves the same leeway as we do others. So the first step is looking at your recording as if you were looking at someone else performing.

As you look at your recording, you want to take small snapshots. Try to focus on small sections as an instructor, breaking it down into small parts just like you would do as the student practicing the skill. One of the marks of a great instructor is the ability to see and correct small issues. Those small things add up to big things when put together. So make sure as you analyze your performance you are detail oriented.

You most definitely should be taking notes. Write down all the things you see that you are doing wrong, as well as all the things you see you are doing right. Don't forget to praise yourself for the good stuff just like you would a student under your guidance!

Once you have notes on the spots you need to work on or the small corrections that need to be made, you are ready to move on to the next "R."

Refine

This is where you will look at your notes you made as the *instructor*, and then apply those as the *student*. Try to fix each thing you noticed when you were reviewing your performance of the skill. But don't try to fix them all at once! You should work on each thing individually, making sure you have corrected it before you move on. Often I see students who have 3 things they should work on and they gloss over them thinking just knowing about them is enough. You need to drill down on exactly what is wrong with your technique, approach, or whatever it is that you noticed.

Once you have worked on each spot that you had noticed, you are ready to take a shot at the next "R."

Repeat

This one might seem like common sense, but the mistake so many people make is they Record, Review, Refine - and then assume it is all fixed. But just like our rock tumbler, it usually takes a couple of times through the cycle to smooth things out. As a matter of fact, sometimes fixing one thing will expose a deeper problem. So this *Repeat* step is essential. Never expect you can notice a problem and just correct it in one simple step. Rather put it to the test by recording again, and then as you review it, look at your previous notes to make sure you fixed the first problem, and see if you notice anything else.

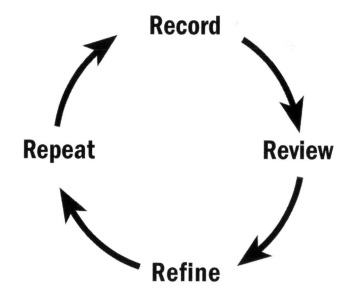

Be diligent about making yourself stick to the Four R Circle

- Record, Review, Refine, Repeat. This system will help you drill down on exactly what you need to work on. It actually also helps you see a slightly different perspective on things as well when you are *The Teacher* instead of *The Student*.

Getting better at any skill is a matter of making small corrections, and gradually polishing your skill to the point of it looking shiny and smooth just like those rocks you can buy in the store!

31: Skill Tree

"It's the little details that are vital. Little things make big things happen." John Wooden

Sometimes it can be difficult figuring out those "little details" that you need to work on at practice. There can be too many options, too many variables, and it can be hard to see all the individual parts. It is feasible, then, that a crucial piece of the practice puzzle can be overlooked.

I often hear students say, "I'm just not sure what to practice on."

A great way to get a handle on what exactly you need to practice as you are mapping out your skill, is to create what I call a *Skill Tree*.

The Skill Tree will give you both the Macro and the Micro of all the elements of the skill. It will show you an overview of all the parts of the skill and how they connect together, and also help you drill down on exactly where you are and what you need to do.

There are a couple of different ways you can create your Skill Tree. You can start with the top level things at the top of the page, and then create the hierarchy tree downward. Another way that some people like to lay it out is as a *mind map* which can not only be a great way to organize the material but can also help you visualize it. Of course you can also simply make a list.

I think it can also really help to think of your Skill Tree as a diagram you might see in your lawn mower manual, or the instructions from that crazy bookshelf you bought. You know the one that you have to assemble, that shows you the million replacement parts you can order. This is called an *exploded view* where you see the parts separately but can also see where they belong in relation to the whole. This can be similar to a mind map, and really helps you tie things together.

I would suggest you do a Skill Tree for every skill you want to get better at. It makes sense to do this alongside of doing your Skillbox Inventory lists as the Tree will actually help you make out your lists and certainly cause you to see the items on your lists in a slightly different way.

The other thing I find when I do a Skill Tree is I almost always end up being able to break the skill down into smaller chunks, giving me more specific things to work on, which of course is much better for getting better!

Often when I have students do a Skill Tree it ends up looking like the Charlie Brown Christmas Tree. Small and sickly! That's because they tend not to drill down deep enough or separate the various parts in fine enough detail.

For example, if someone is making a Skill Tree of what they need to practice for baseball they may tell me, "Well, I need to work on throwing and catching and hitting. Those are the three branches of my Skill Tree." Like I said, Charlie Brown.

Even if we kept the top level pretty simple, we might

divide it up into catching, throwing, hitting, running, and the mental game. But take a look at how I would fill out just one of the branches of the tree from there. I would certainly break each section into as much detail as possible. But if I just write out how I would breakdown the various skills I would practice for "catching," you can see the branch gets pretty bushy pretty fast!

Catching

- Pop Fly - Long - Short
- Line Drives
- Fielding grounders - off of grass - off of dirt
- Hard throws
- Soft throws
- Bare handed
- Reaching to the left side of body
- Reaching to the right side of body
- While running - left - right - forward - backward
- Diving in all directions
- Catching under lights at night
- From different areas on the field

Then systematically do all of the above in every different environmental condition - wind - no wind - sun - partial sun - cloudy - light rain - dew on ground - super hot - super cold

In practicing just "catching" vs practicing all the details of catching I have listed, which do you think would give you the most complete workout of that part of the skill of baseball? If you had to pick someone to be on your team, would you pick Player A who has been practicing the simple top level "catching," or player B who has been digging deep working on each tiny little aspect of catching?

I believe just going by their practice regimen the logical choice would be clear.

Start building out your Skill Tree by deciding what are the top level categories of your skill then drill down until you get to the micro level. Then look sideways, and see if it can get even further refined in a slightly different way. This will give you the practice map you need, and a great *view* of all the elements of your skill.

32: **1%**

Legendary Lakers coach Pat Riley wrote about it in his book *The Winner Within.*

Cycling coach Dave Brailsford led the British cycling *Team Sky* to win the Tour De France using this method.

Many others have espoused similar philosophies in books like *The Slight Edge* or *The Compound Effect.*

So what is this secret method that many have used successfully?

The idea that the way to get better at something is to do it in very small increments. Baby steps.

We tend to always look at the end result we want, and it is often a large leap from where we are. The problem lies in getting there. When a goal or achievement target is too far off, it can discourage us from even starting on a path to get there. We end up defeated before we even start!

Our brains tell us we need a BIG solution. We need to go from 0 to 60 mph in 1 second! We don't want to have to save pennies a day, we would rather just win the lottery. That is how we are wired up - we want the big score all at once - and all RIGHT NOW. But rarely do big things come all at once. The *overnight sensation* only exists in the movies. Most real life overnight successes take years.

So what should we do? Just make small goals? Never "shoot for the moon"? Keep our plans conservative? As with almost everything you will find me talking about when it comes to getting better at anything, the key is having a system. In this case the answer is not to shrink your goals, but rather to keep your focus on small improvements across a wide range of elements that will then add up to a huge leap.

Over the years I have worked with and interviewed people who have achieved massive success in a variety of fields, and the one common thread is that they have all put together a long string of little steps to get there!

Coach Riley talked about how the Lakers had stumbled in the 1986 season, mostly due to complacency after having beat their nemesis the Celtics in 1985. As Riley puts it, "Even Kareem who was our team captain said 'How can we top that'? That was when I knew we had a problem."

So for the '87 season, Riley came up with a plan. He would just ask players to improve 1% in each of 5 selected areas. Seems simple. "The players took a look at this one percent and said, 'Oh, I can improve one percent in anything.'" So if a player was averaging 8 rebounds a game, now they just needed to average 8.08. But, when you put all of those gains together spread across 12 players - that is a huge leap forward. And that was what they did.

Riley says they tracked these numbers without fail. "We had it computerized and we'd spit out the numbers every day. So, they knew exactly where they were and that it wasn't just lip service. It allowed them to see where they stood and how they were doing. We did it every single day until we achieved a change."[1]

And achieve a change they did. Now back on track, they not only won the '87 championship, but went on to win it in '88 as well, making them the first team in 19 years to win back to back championships. All from tiny little improvements.

Coach Dave Brailsford from the British cycling team *Team Sky* was up against a challenge. No British rider had ever won the Tour De France. Heck they had only recently won their first really big event in the last 97 years! Yeah, that's a challenge. "OK guys, I know it's been 97 years, but I think we have a chance".... Probably wouldn't have went over too well as a pep talk. But Coach Dave had a different plan. In his words: "The whole principle came from the idea that if you broke down everything you could think of that goes into riding a bike, and then improved it by 1%, you will get a significant increase when you put them all together."[2]

Ah, it's that pesky 1% thing again. Sure seems easy when you look at it that way. Dave called this principle, "The aggregation of marginal gains." I would imagine that other teams would come to know this as "The aggravation of marginal gains" because it worked so well.

It was downright science!

Team Sky looked into each element of the rider's life - hired nutritionists to look at each person's dietary needs - broke down each part of a bicycle per each rider's specific needs and exact size - researched which pillow was the best for sleeping and then not only brought those for each rider, but brought the riders own bed into each hotel room they stayed at for better sleep. They basically went through every miniscule detail of each rider's life and asked, "How can we make it 1% better?"

Of course with all of these 1% targets, sometimes you overshoot, and get better by 2, or 5, or 20% thereby making huge gains when you put it all together.

It worked. The British won the Tour De France in 2012, 2013, 2015, 2016 and 2017. Dave's system has been adopted by most everyone else as well. If you think that just getting on a bike and riding will get you to the top now - sorry, those days are over thanks to the aggregation of marginal gains.

Could this work for other things? Could this work for YOU?

I know for a fact that this will work for anything you want to get better at in your life.

What if you took any skill you wanted to get better at and broke it down into small sections, and then just looked at getting 1% better in each of those areas? Now that could work. 1% improvement is easy, very reachable . The very effort to just get a little better at one small thing is bound to also inspire you to work hard at it since it seems like something that can really happen. Unlike some goals that seem out of reach, the 1% concept should help build confidence in what you can achieve.

Let's take the game of the average weekend tennis player. What if they decided to improve their 1st serve percentage by 1%, their return percentage by 1%, serve speed by 1%, footwork consistency by 1%, and backhand power by 1%. You get the idea. There would be a lot of individual things just in the actual playing that could improve by those slight margins. Then compound it all by diving into tiny improvements in shoes, rackets, sunglasses, diet, sleep, workouts, and the list goes on. Now if you add all of those things up, you get an amazing increase in the overall skill level. Even if you fail to improve some areas at all, you will most likely improve others by quite a bit. The numbers don't lie. Getting just a little better in several areas is not as trivial as it may sound!

Try it out for yourself.

1. Pick a skill, break it into 5 to 7 areas that you could improve upon independently, and then tackle getting just 1% better in each of those areas.

2. Track your progress! This is the key to not only being able to see what is working, but also to motivate yourself with tiny steps to your goal of 1% in each area!

3. Be willing to shift your focus between the different areas you are trying to improve based on what is working and what needs a little extra attention.

If you apply this method of improving various elements of your skill by 1% each, I guarantee you will find it easier to succeed than you thought, and once you add it all up, you just might be surprised at the magical big leap you will have taken!

33: Right, Wrong, Right

Have you ever been practicing something and it just *felt* right? The movements were all in sync so the sequence of it was all flowing. You could just tell this was it. You were in the zone.

With anything that is tactile or anything that is movement based, being able to *feel* when it is right can really help focus your practice.

So when practicing, one technique I find very helpful is what I call the *Right, Wrong, Right* method. You will do something several times the right way, but then make yourself do it wrong.

If you are playing guitar maybe that means with your hand in a weird position, or a bad fingering pattern. If you are working on your golf swing you might lift one foot off the ground or switch your hands on your grip. If you are working on a new language you might say some words with your tongue sticking out the corner of your mouth! But just do it wrong a couple of times.

Then immediately notice what the *wrong* element is, and correct it and do it right several times paying special attention to the part that you just corrected. This will help you know when it *feels right.* You will find that you become very comfortable doing it right and when you do it wrong a warning goes off in your head because you have learned what wrong is!

In his book *The Talent Code*, Daniel Coyle outlines one of the main teaching techniques in the arsenal of legendary UCLA basketball coach John Wooden. "One of Wooden's most frequent forms of teaching was a three-part instruction where he modeled the right way to do something, showed the incorrect way, and then remodeled the right way."[1] There is no doubt that Coach Wooden knew a thing or two about building excellent skills. Using this Right, Wrong, Right method will work for what you are practicing just as well as it did on his 10 time National championship winning players.

Remember, excellence in any skill is built by stacking small changes and corrections together to form the right way. Just like every little brick contributes to building a huge apartment building, so it is with each time you reinforce in your mind what the *right* movement or thought is. You are just laying another brick in the foundation of your skill.

The next time you practice, use the *Right, Wrong, Right* method and you will start to establish clear lines between the right way and the wrong way. That way you will make sure you are spending your practice energy in the right places!

34: Practice it Like You Will Perform it

When wide receiver Odell Beckham Jr. burst onto the professional football scene after being drafted by the NY Giants, he was described as a phenom. Odell has since caused quite a stir with both his on and off field activities.

Even in the middle of breaking record after record, the highlight that made the national spotlight was his amazing one handed catch during a *Sunday Night Football* game against the Dallas Cowboys. This catch that was made as Odell was falling backwards into the endzone for a touchdown made every highlight reel on every sports show across the country, and was called by many the greatest catch of all time.

But was it indeed a "miracle catch?" Well, it was certainly amazing, but maybe not that miraculous. Upon further investigation, it seems Odell can be seen on the field before every game practicing what? You guessed it: One handed catches.

While that catch looked practically impossible to us mere mortals, the reality is that Odell catches a lot of those in practice. This one just happened to be in the middle of a nationally televised game, in prime time, for a touchdown. But for Odell, it was just business as usual.

We tend to have this same reaction when we see anyone do something that is so far above what the normal person can do. Our minds grapple with the only explanation we can muster. It has to be a miracle.

It's like watching world class Table Tennis (Ping Pong) players. The ball moves so fast that it seems impossible that they can track and hit it at all let alone put it back onto the table in the right place with the right spin. To do that over and over again is hard to fathom. When we watch extreme sports athletes do multiple back flips on motorcycles or snowmobiles, or see snowboarders and skiers hit a jump and flip and twist and spin all while barreling downhill, it seems like a miracle. But to all of these folks, it is closer to business as usual. It's just what they do.

What can we learn from all of this that will help us in our practice?

Odell didn't just accidentally make that catch during the game. He was able to pull that off because he had prepared for it by using one of the most important concepts I can teach you. *Practice it like you are going to perform it.*

If you practice one way, and then step on the field or stage and expect to get completely different results, you will be disappointed. You have to do it in practice just like you will do it when it counts.

Performance Situation Practicing

I call this type of practice *Performance Situation Practicing* or PSP. Nothing will prepare you for game time like working through everything you might encounter beforehand during practice.

I have seen guitar students struggle with this for years. They can play a song really well sitting in their comfy office chair with headphones on at a low volume, but put them on stage and it can be a different story.

On stage they are standing instead of sitting. They have a loud amp and drums blasting in their ears and bright lights in their eyes. They are playing in front of people instead of alone in the comfort of their own home with an audience of none. These different conditions can make the simplest song suddenly seem impossible to play.

In order to prepare for being on stage they need to make sure they put themselves in as close to those situations as they can during practice.

When I am practicing my disc dog game of Toss and Catch (where you have one minute to see how many 40 yard catches your dog can make) I often practice without my dog so I can work on my throws. However, I am always visualizing my dog being there. I call her name and encourage her to come back fast after the throw. I act out taking the disc from her and yell "Go, Go, Go" as I am throwing to encourage her to run down the field.

I do this while I am out there all by myself. Granted, I am sure my neighbors originally thought I was crazy shouting to the imaginary dog in my yard, but they are probably used to it by now. It is important to create a scenario as close to the real thing as I can, and if that makes me weird so be it. Practice it like you are going to perform it.

There are two important areas to focus on with PSP. The actual skill itself, and the context or environment that the skill is performed in. Both are extremely valuable to work on and complement each other.

1. SKILL SIMULATION

Practice things such as the mechanics of what you are working on, the repeatable motions, the mental processes. If you are a golfer you work on things like keeping your back swing smooth as you practice your long drive visualizing the green in the distance. Pay attention to the motion and hit points that you will encounter on every tee box.

2. CONTEXT/ENVIRONMENT SIMULATION

To practice the context that your skill will be used in, you may practice your golf shots from deep in the sand in the bunker. Or if the skill you are working on is one that is done under the pressure of time, make sure that you have a timer running. Or if there are some unique physical conditions you will have to perform under, make sure you spend some time in that mode during practice.

Take whatever you can from the performance situation and *do it like that* when you practice.

If you have spent enough time practicing in game mode, then when you jump up on stage and play the song perfectly, and look like you have done it a million times, it is no surprise. Or when time is running out in a competition and that last throw to my dog comes off as effortless even under pressure, it isn't that big of a deal. As a matter of fact it is exactly what I expect – because that is how I have practiced it. Business as usual.

This has an amazing impact on your mental game as practicing performance situations will make you much more comfortable and relaxed during the real thing.

Performance Situation Practicing not only helps motor

skills and your mental game, but it also helps you avoid frustration and keeps practice fun! The closer you simulate game time scenarios during your practice, the more effective your practice will be at preparing you for crunch time.

I have also seen this "Miracle Catch" phenomenon come into play in my musical career. When my band was touring, there was one song in particular that had a section full of stops and starts, riffs and licks. All coordinated between myself and my drummer and bass player. We all hit stops together, had synchronized riffs and played this very tight section exactly the same each night.

Many people would come up after the show and that was the song that they would comment on. "Wow, I can't believe how you guys could play that so perfectly together"...Or "Sounded like you guys were just magically in each other's minds and knew what the other guy was going to play."

The thing about it was, that for us, it was one of the easier sections of the night. Why? Because we had rehearsed those stops and licks a million times. We had that section down and did it the same every time. We had prepared it for *game time* and done it just like we would on stage.

Of course as musicians that love to improvise we always get excited about playing the parts that we haven't worked out, where we get to push our musical boundaries together. But for really getting "ready for the game", there is no substitute for repeatedly practicing it like you are going to perform it.

To those in the audience, the rehearsed start and stop section seemed like the hardest thing. For us it was business as usual.

So the next time you practice, be sure to include simulating game time scenarios for some of your practice session. Work on Performance Situation Practicing in order to prepare yourself for when it's time to shine! That way when it is time to perform you will make those amazing moves look easy, because that is the way you have been practicing it, just like Odell.

Practice it like you are going to perform it, and it will turn "miracles" into business as usual.

35: Super Slo-Mo

A technique that I have seen work across a wide range of different skills is what I call the *Super Slo-Mo*. This is really best if the skill you are working on is movement based, but that movement can be anything from a golf swing to forming words while learning a new language.

The thing you want to convince yourself of when doing this is to practice 5 times slower than you normally do. This is much easier said than done! We all have a tendency to get locked into our own speed when working on things. Some of us tend to do things at a faster speed and some at a slower pace, but one thing I notice working with students is they all have their individual *normal* range.

Most of us will slow something down when it isn't working or we want to see exactly what is happening. But usually, we simply run through it a time or two and then we think we have it.

The Super Slo-Mo technique is a little different.

This method is to take something that you are practicing on and do it as you normally would, at regular speed, for a few repetitions or a few minutes, Then, do it a couple of times really slow in Super Slo-Mo, paying close attention to the technique. When I say really slow I mean like almost standing still Super Slo-Mo, barely moving. After a couple of times through in Super Slo-Mo, immediately go right back to normal speed for a couple more reps. This is just a great habit to get into regardless of what you are working on.

The key is while you are doing it slow you need to pay attention to any little shifts, or changes in feel, or any little thing that you might want to change when you go back up to speed. Sometimes just analyzing it as you do it slowly can help you improve your feel.

So unlike just slowing it down, going Super Slo-Mo can help make things clear. This is especially true when you get something down pretty well but are having trouble taking it to the very top level. Stop, slow down and really focus on your technique.

This might seem like a really simple technique, but most things that are effective are simple. The next time you practice, use the Super Slo-Mo technique a few times and see if it shows you things about what you are practicing that you may have been overlooking.

36: The Edge

"You are not trying Jef-fu-son!" This was the summation from my instructor Mr. Pak. "But I am trying," I replied. To which he just smiled. You really couldn't argue with Mr. Pak. Once he had given instruction, no matter how much I tried to defend or justify my ineptness, my retort was always just met with a smile. Such is the way of the master and the grasshopper.

Grandmaster Pak was my Taekwondo instructor. He held 8th degree black belts in both Taekwondo and Hapkido, and a 6th degree black belt in Judo. Suffice it to say he knew what he was talking about. His verbal instructions were very measured and sparse. He preferred to let his one liners just percolate in your brain.

He called me "Jef-fu-son" from day one, and just saying my name like that could be all that was needed to get his point across. I recall on more than one occasion where during a sparring session between myself and another student he would stop us and step in between us. Then with his eyes closed and his head held down slowly shaking side to side, he would just say "Jef-fu-son." That clearly and completely told me what he was thinking, without him having to actually say, "That was awful!"

Back to when he told me I wasn't trying. It was as I attempted to do a spinning wheel kick to break a board. A board was being held by another student a few feet in front of me about a foot above my head. My job was to spin 360 degrees, as I leapt in the air with my right leg over my head coming around with enough velocity and accuracy to break the board. I would try and either fall down, or almost kill my fellow student with a wild kick. Mr. Pak simply said we would "fix." The problem was that I wasn't convinced I was ready for this. I didn't think I was quite good enough.

Over the next couple of weeks he didn't have me attempt to break the board, but he had me work on the move. His assessment was I was not stretching fully and what he called "reaching to the edge" with my leg. I was too afraid I would fall down so I pulled my leg back. He helped me overcome that by having another student hold on to me and have me stretch my leg out as far as I could in the movement. There is a commitment you have to make when you do moves like this. Basically an all or nothing kind of attitude is what you need to have. He helped me get comfortable doing it with the other students providing a bit of a safety net by holding on to me.

This is the same way many Xtreme sports athletes get used to new tricks. Whether it's back flips on a motorcycle or a snowboarder doing a 1260 double McTwist, it usually starts out with them doing the trick as they jump into a giant pit filled with foam. Once they have the confidence to lay it all on the line in the foam, then they take it to the jump or the slope.

So it was with my wheel kick. Mr. Pak knew I was holding back and doing it too safe. So he had to get me to practice the move out "on the edge" of my ability. Once that became comfortable, then actually doing it would be no big deal.

After two weeks of practicing it with help, trying to stretch myself and following through with the words "let go" that he told me over and over throughout the time I studied with him, I was ready. My fellow student held the board up, I stepped up, spun, kicked and *snap* the board split cleanly. What was once beyond my ability now was within it. I had gotten there by working on the edge of my skill set until the edge moved closer to the center and now there was a new edge.

That is how any skill works. The edge is only the edge until you can do it. Then it is no longer the edge.

Antoine de Saint-Exupéry said, "Only the unknown frightens men. But once a man has faced the unknown, that terror becomes the known." So it is with chipping away at those things that lie on the outer edge of your skill. But there is more to it than that. Practicing on the edge of your ability not only makes the stuff on the edge possible, it is in fact the only way to grow.

In his book *The Talent Code*, Daniel Coyle says, "Struggling in certain targeted ways, operating at the edges of your ability, where you make mistakes - makes you smarter."[1]

This makes sense. We know that our biggest gains come from doing something, noticing problems, making small corrections and repeating the process. So the edge gives us the most opportunities to do things wrong, thereby giving us the maximum number of small corrections we can apply. This *trying - failing - fixing* series of steps eventually builds a great foundation for any skill.

The idea of working out there on the edge of your ability is really fundamental to everything you have learned since you first attempted to walk as a toddler. You push and push and then breakthrough. Then it's on to the next thing. That's why you aren't just sitting there on the floor as an adult!

Our practice stagnates when we fall into the trap of just

continuing to do the same things over and over that we already have down. I used to tell advanced guitar students there was no sense in spending 3 hours practicing that open G chord they learned when they first started playing. That won't make you better. You need to practice the things you can't do, until they become the things you can do.

This is where the three Skillbox inventory lists help you determine what you should be working on at any given time. You want to make sure you are spending the biggest chunk of your practice time in the most effective way. Always strive to work on the edge of your skill.

Some call this the *learning edge*, some call it the *growing edge*, but the fact remains that out there on the edge is where you can see new opportunities and test what you are capable of.

Or as Kurt Vonnegut put it, "I want to stand as close to the edge as I can without going over. Out on the edge you see all kinds of things you can't see from the center."

It is so easy to just stay safe, keep in the comfort zone where you go through the motions of practice and then feel good about yourself because you feel like you put in your time practicing. However, that will eventually cause frustration when you don't see the results of improvement that you had hoped for. You have to consciously remind yourself to spend a good amount of your practice time out there on the edge of your ability.

Get in the habit of checking your work to make sure you are spending time on the edge.

37: Bump the Ceiling

Speed is a desirable quality in many skills. Any kind of race or timed event has a speed element to it. We love things that go fast. Hotdog eating contests are not based on how slowly you can eat them. And while Aesop's Tortoise did beat the Hare to the finish line, we know it was the Hare's nap and wrong strategy that was at fault, not his outright speed!

Most sports, even if they are not directly dependent on a player's top speed, are favorable to players who are quick and have general speed.

Former NFL player Donovin Darius said, "In all my 25 plus years of competitive athletics, I've never heard someone get released or cut from a team because they were too fast."

There are certainly many ways to look at the speed of an athlete. Whether it is watching a tennis pro's footwork, the punching quickness of an MMA fighter's strikes, or the stride of a sprinter, all these movements are fed by fast twitch muscle fibers.

Your fast twitch muscle fibers are responsible for quick muscle contractions, whereas your slow twitch fibers are more involved in endurance and can sustain activity for longer periods. Of course focusing on drills and exercises specific to your skill to help you isolate and train these specific muscles is one way to tackle speed.

The other thing I want to talk about when it comes to increasing your speed, will also help us with getting better at anything. It is this concept I call *Bump the Ceiling*.

In the world of guitar students, one topic comes up over and over again. How can I play faster? This is understandable as most students hear these amazing guitar solos ripping from the fingers of their favorite guitar heroes and want to play like that. But gaining speed on guitar can be just as difficult as gaining speed on your golf swing or your left hook!

I have seen it over and over again where students get frustrated because their speed is not increasing. Many times this can be traced back to how they are practicing, not just what they are practicing. If you always practice in your *comfort zone* where you can pull it off without any problem, then you are not really out there on the edge where you need to be. This becomes a glaring issue when we are talking about speed, because that is often measurable!

For example if you are a musician practicing scales, you can look at your metronome setting and see what tempo you are at. If you can play a piece of music at 120 beats per minute today, then you can check your setting tomorrow and push it up to 122. Then 125 and so on. The key of course is tracking it, and then increasing it.

However, I think a key ingredient to increasing speed is not only to do it a *little* faster each time, but occasionally do it as fast as you possibly can. Even if it gets sloppy and you drive in the ditch, you need to flirt with what it feels like to really step it up. You need to bump your head on the ceiling to find out where it is!

Push it to your limit, then slow it back down and gain control and start working on the process again. But if you never push it to the breaking point, you won't really know what is possible.

T.S. Eliot said, "Only those who will risk going too far, can possibly find out how far one can go."

So it is with the idea of bumping the ceiling. This also puts you by default out there on the edge of your ability which we have already determined is the best spot to grow overall.

So if you are trying to gain speed on your golf swing, practice it the normal way, working on what you need to do, but then occasionally just try to go as fast as you can. Don't worry about technique or any other things you have had your mind on regarding your swing. Just put all your focus on the one task of going as fast as you can right now.

That by itself can be an eye opener when you feel that speed. You will likely think, "Wow, if I could get that much club speed AND keep my accuracy, I could be a contender!" Well, yes, that's the idea anyway. Get a taste of what it feels like, and then work towards that.

The other thing that can help you solidify what speed can do, is to get around someone who is fast. It's not the same when you watch someone on YouTube or see them from a distance. But when you are right next to a Disc Golfer who is throwing a Frisbee 500 feet, you see and feel the arm speed it takes to propel a disc that far. The first time I was next to someone who could throw bombs, the first thought in my head was "Wow! My arm needs to go faster!" That gives you a great way to gauge what is needed as well.

The secret with this *Bump the Ceiling* concept is to know where your ceiling actually is, and then where your safe and controlled spot is so you can go back and forth between them. With a little practice you will be able to take anything you are working on and *push* it to the edge, and then slow it back down to where you can play it perfectly. Gradually bumping your head on your ceiling of ability will cause the ceiling to rise!

38: Play it Backwards

I will never forget the first time someone told me to play a guitar lick backwards. It was just a simple blues lick, but it was hard! None of the natural movements that I had in my muscle memory were helping, and none of the *guitaristic* techniques that I could play in my sleep worked! Everything was backwards. I really had to think about it!

I find that if you take any movement based skill and spend a little time trying to play parts of it, or the whole thing backwards, it can be very beneficial to your development.

We spend a ton of time getting things in our muscle memory. We move things from the conscious to the sub-conscious. This is all done for good reason. We need that *auto* movement to make things smooth. However, sometimes that also makes it hard to look at things critically and analyze if it is the most efficient way to do it, once it is ingrained so deeply. Flipping things over and doing it backwards can expose spots that you may not have been able to see.

Take the example, of shooting a free throw in basketball. If you go through the movement backwards, you might see that your release could be a little more vertical, or your shoulders should be squared up more. This stuff is hard to see or feel doing it the normal way up to speed.

Try it. Take any movement based skill and do it backwards. It will likely have to be slower as well since it will feel a little strange. But seeing movements from a different perspective can help trigger some new thought on how to improve.

Make a habit of doing something backwards during each practice session. Then consider if there is anything you discovered that warrants further critiquing.

39: Play in the Dark

I recall as a boy taking a family vacation that included a tour through Marvel Cave in Branson, MO. We walked into this large cave entrance with stalagmites, stalactites, and all manner of interesting underground formations. We then continued down a long tunnel with lights running all along the sides. About halfway down, the tour guide told us not to move and then proceeded to shut off the lights. It was completely dark. This was of course before everyone had a cel phone, so there was no glow from devices - just utter darkness.

Once a few gasps and some muttering from the tourists had calmed down, our guide told us to be as quiet as we could and just listen. It was like our ears all of a sudden came to life! The same drips of water and various sounds that had gone completely unnoticed before when the lights were on, now sounded loud and clear! I remember being pretty impressed with how my hearing suddenly *improved* and I heard in much greater detail.

This of course isn't as much instant improvement as it is just shifting your sense's focus. When you don't have all that information coming into your brain from your eyes, you have more resources to apply to other senses. Over time, according to studies in *The Journal of Neuroscience*, blind people's brains can actually rewire themselves to make up for the lack of sight. This *Neuroplasticity* or ability of the brain to change because of experience might not have exactly been the cause of me hearing better in the cave, but there is no doubt my body has an amazing capacity to adapt!

That episode in the cave did teach me to shift focus to my ears later in life when I became a musician. You have most likely seen your favorite musician shut their eyes in the middle of a particularly emotional passage. That's just a way for them to put all their focus on the auditory aspect of what they are doing, and it works!

We can use this cool sensory improvement hack in our practicing. While you can just close your eyes, I suggest sitting in a room that is completely dark. It has to be so dark that you can't see your hand in front of your face. You may have to do some quick explaining of this part of your practice session when your spouse or parent opens the door to you sitting in the dark... but it will be worth it.

Anything you can safely do in the pitch black of a windowless room with the lights out can help you attack the skill in a whole new way.

All skills requiring hearing, work great with this technique. All kinds of music practice, language learning, public speaking rehearsals, they all benefit from improved auditory senses.

However, you might also find that things requiring movements, such as a tennis swing, or a dance step, can take on a different feel in the dark. Once again, because you can't *see* where your forearm is in relation to your hips, you have to *feel* it. This way of going through motions that you may have been relying on sight to complete takes on a whole new dimension when the lights are out!

When you have a chance, and it's possible, try to work on your skill in the dark.

40: Play Like Carl

We are all familiar with the classic scene in *Caddyshack* where Carl the greenskeeper is whacking away at the country club's flowers. He is simultaneously playing the voice of the commentator calling the game, and the young golfer. "Cinderella story, out of nowhere, a former greenskeeper...and now, about to become the Masters Champion."

Most of us did some form of this when we were kids. Whether we were out shooting baskets and counting down the final 10 seconds as Larry Bird took the game winning shot, or if we were playing with dolls and "talking" our way through various scenes.

Being your own commentator can also be helpful when working on a variety of skills.

This is a form of *self talk* which is really just psychologists way of giving a name to what goes through all of our heads most of the time. Self talk can be positive, "You are going to ace this test," or negative, "You will NEVER pass this test, why even try."

The key is harnessing this self talk and controlling what exactly you say. It has been proven that positive self talk can boost your confidence and help focus your performance, which is helpful when working on skill development. Of course negative self talk can be traced back to countless losses, flubs and complete breakdowns. Many times when you see someone *choke* during a big moment, there is a good chance that the conversation going on in their head right before that happened wasn't on the positive side!

When we look at trying to pump ourselves up with positive self talk, one thing to remember is we are pretty good at knowing the difference between what's really possible and plain old fluff. So if things look bleak, maybe instead of "Don't worry, it will work out great!" you might want to try a realistic approach like, "Let's look at some options we have to make this better."

Keeping things attainable instead of unrealistic will build up your belief in the concept over time. Self talk is like a muscle. You need to build it up gradually and keep working it.

One of the important aspects of self talk is each person is unique, and your mind might react better to direct, coach like instruction. Or it could work better with a kinder, gentler approach. Just keep it positive and experiment to see what works for you.

For some people, self talk that takes more of a *coaching* tone is helpful. Even addressing yourself in the third person, which can seem a little weird in normal conversation with others, can help create distance between you and your self talk, treating it more like advice to a friend.

I might say, "Jeff, just relax when you step up to the line and take a deep breath," before I start a competition round with my dog. That can be more calming than telling myself, "I need to relax at the line and take a deep breath." Anything with "I" in it can put pressure on yourself studies have shown. We have all said, "I am going to…" way too many times and then not actually followed through with what we said we were going to do. So our minds get wise to our ways and realize that, "I need to relax" is just another one of those things I probably won't follow through with. However, giving someone good advice, even if it is yourself, can feel more genuine.

Many times people think any kind of positive self talk or visualization is only for when you are at the competition or performing. That is not true! It can be a tremendous help for your practice!

Setting yourself up with phrases as you practice such as, "It's normal for me to hit this ball right down the middle of the fairway in this situation," or "The nerves I feel before this speech are because I am excited for how good it will be," will help your practice time pay off.

One of the things I see happen with people who go out to practice something, is they don't have their head in the game. They are just sort of going through the motions. I find that a little self talk in a positive way can really help me concentrate on what I am doing and treat it a bit more serious.

Some tips for using self talk successfully during practice.

1. Start by acknowledging that your self talk can help or hurt your practice. Then pay attention to how and when you are doing it.

2. Keep it positive. Rather than telling yourself, "Don't miss this shot," say "I am making this shot."

3. Combine self talk with good visualization and images

for more powerful impact. For example see yourself hitting the golf ball perfectly down the fairway as you say, "That is the way I will hit it."

4.   Once you come up with certain cue words or phrases that click for you and seem to work, stick with those to boost your performance.

5.   Keep it fun. Don't take yourself too seriously, and feel free to break into Carl's commentator mode occasionally to keep yourself smiling!

41: 5 Times Perfect

This is *gamification* at it's finest. Reach the goal before you can move on to the next level. I use this with students all the time. I also find it especially helpful for a student who is struggling to get something down.

The technique is simply this: Do whatever you are working on perfectly 5 times in a row before you move on. That sounds simple, but if you keep making a mistake on the fifth time through it can get pretty frustrating! This will tend to make you really focus. There is nothing like the fear of potentially having to do the same thing over and over again for the next 3 hours to make you focus and get it right!

This works best with simple and small skills, or parts of larger skills.

You may be annunciating and timing the delivery of a certain line in a speech you are giving, so nail it 5 times perfect before you move on. You may be kicking a soccer ball on a penalty kick and bending it into the upper left hand corner of the goal. Same thing here, you have to kick it 5 times perfect before you move on. You may be a model working on your turn on the runway so do it 5 times perfect before you move on.

If you are working on something that is out there on the

edge of your ability, it may be harder than you think to nail it 5 times in a row. If you are struggling, just relax and look at the smallest components of the skill you can. Then work on each little piece or any transitions that are giving you trouble and then try again.

I have had students break out in a sweat even before we started this anticipating their failure in completing it 5 times! That pressure is also a good thing to work on, it is just like a performance! You gotta be able to do it right when it counts.

Try the 5 times perfect method the next time you are working on something and see if it doesn't help you pull your effort into focus.

42: Perspective

As I sat there in my chair, I looked down at the magazine lying on the floor. It was leaning against a stack of books and bent in the middle. The cover featured a picture of Tim Ferriss, author of the *4 Hour Workweek*, and life experimenter extraordinaire.

When I looked at it I thought "Man, Tim looks angry on that cover." Then I picked the magazine up and it flattened out and I saw the *normal* Tim. It was so weird how this difference of the magazine's orientation completely changed his look and the vibe. I found myself having to bend it and flatten it several times. Going back and forth from the angry Tim to the normal Tim made me laugh (It's true I have a pretty warped sense of humor.)

This shows us how just looking at something with a different perspective can totally change our perception of it.

We've all been in a situation; political discussion, sports debate, conversation with our spouse, that has shown us that two people can interpret the exact same situation in completely different ways. Both people are 100% convinced their way of seeing it is the *right* way and they can't believe the other person can't see it.

Perspective is powerful.

Could the perspective you have of yourself and your ability to get better at something have an impact on whether or not you actually get better?

As a matter of fact it could.

Sian Beilock is a psychology professor at The University of Chicago, and one of her research studies looked at success and failures in students taking math tests. She says, "We found that cortisol, a hormone released in response to stress, can either be tied to a student's poor performance on a math test or contribute to success, depending on the frame of mind of the student going into the test."[1]

So basically, even the physiological effects of stress can be used for good or bad depending on your perspective of how well you are going to do. You are pre-determining the outcome!

Your perspective on what and how you are actually practicing can also help or hinder your efforts. Sometimes it helps to see a larger picture of what you are working on so you can see every detail.

NASCAR drivers have a unique but somewhat limited perspective of what is happening during a race. They see the track in front of them, and a small shot of what is going on behind them in their rearview mirror. But due to the HANS device (which stands for Head and Neck Support) along with their helmet, it makes it difficult for the drivers to see to the sides of their cars. It's not like driving down the freeway in the family SUV where a quick glance over your right shoulder can let you know it is clear to move over a lane.

To compensate for their limited vision, each driver has a *spotter*. The spotter is a person who sits up on top of the grandstand and communicates to the driver via radio, telling them all the info they need and filling in gaps in their perspective. A spotter can see the whole track and has to be quick to tell a driver when there is someone on his outside quarter panel, or when a driver passes a car, the spotter tells him when it is *clear*, meaning when he can pull over in front of that car. Think about how stressful it would be to not be able to see what is to your left or right driving down the interstate if you need to change lanes. Now think of what that's like at 200 miles per hour.

The spotter has more of an overview or overall perspective of what is going on in the race. They can tell a driver who is behind them, or how many cars are between them and the leader. This is great information to have.

We Could all use that kind of information about a skill we are practicing! Have someone tell us, "Great job, you are moving up, you are about to pass a milestone in two more practices. Don't look over your shoulder, just keep focused on what's in front of you and get up on the wheel and keep your foot on the gas!"

Be your own spotter.

Having a bigger or more complete perspective on something we are trying to get better at can help us see what is working and what is not. This helps give us the confidence to know that we can do this! Think about being your own *spotter*, where you step outside yourself and go up to the top of the grandstand and watch yourself practice. What do you see yourself doing? What would you tell yourself? "Hey, you are rushing through that. Do another set of reps. Add some variation to that. Good job, you are making progress!"

In order to know what to do next, you need to step outside yourself and examine exactly where you are now.

Changing our perspective on the potential we have to get better and on how we see what we practice can be a powerful tool to help things click for us. If our perspective is that we can definitely get better if we practice the right things in the right way, we'll be more likely to want to practice (because we believe it will pay off), and put the time into making sure we are practicing in the most effective way.

Do a *perspective check* the next time you think about your skill and make sure you are seeing things in the best possible way. Don't let a bad perspective ruin your ability to improve.

In one of my favorite movies, *Ratatouille*, nasty villain and food critic Anton Ego goes into Gusteau's restaurant to see if there is any truth to all the rave reviews on the new Chef. Anton would much rather see the place shut down and knows he has the power to influence that with a bad review.

He puts in his order with as much condescension and arrogance as he can muster.

Waiter: Do you know what you'd like this evening, sir?
Anton Ego: Yes, I think I do. After reading a lot of overheated puffery about your new cook, you know what I'm craving? A little perspective. That's it. I'd like some fresh, clear, well seasoned perspective. Can you suggest a good wine to go with that?
Waiter: With what, sir?
Anton Ego: Perspective. Fresh out, I take it?

Waiter: I am, uh...

Anton Ego: Very well. Since you're all out of perspective and no one else seems to have it in this bloody town, I'll make you a deal. You provide the food, I'll provide the perspective.... which would go nicely with a bottle of Cheval Blanc 1947.

Many times that is the way we tend to think. We are waiting for our own Anton to come in, sit down, and provide us with perspective. When actually, we have the ability to create or change our own perspective right now.

While we can get perspective from a great coach, a teacher or mentor, we can also craft it for ourselves! Don't wait for someone else to give you the perspective on getting better at a skill, take stock in yourself, be your own spotter and look at how and what you are practicing and then adjust if needed!

It all starts with your perspective on yourself - how you see yourself. Make a commitment to have the positive perspective that you CAN and WILL get better through practice, and then dig in!

43: **Bored?**

Are you bored with practice? Need some inspiration? Here are 10 things to do right now to shake things up.

1. Call a friend and ask them to get together to practice.
2. Change your position! If you practice sitting down, stand and practice if you can. Or move to a different angle when you stand. Practice with bent knees or straight knees - sit in a different chair - just change it up!
3. Change where you practice for a day - do it on the deck or roof.
4. Go see someone who is already good! Nothing makes you want to get great like seeing greatness!
5. Organize your practice material! Whether you want to or not - it will get you in the groove again!
6. Look at and focus on your goals list. Practice will get you there.
7. Buy a new piece of gear! New stuff always makes practice fun.
8. Create a new piece of gear for practice. Build something! This is similar to above but without the spousal disapproval.

9. Work on a different skill. Practicing piano? Play the drums. Practicing soccer? Shoot some baskets.

10. Watch a recording of yourself from months or years ago. Practice made you better!

Bonus Tip:

The bonus tip is this: Make it fun! Don't stress out over it, just enjoy!

44: Gratitude

"Piglet noticed that even though he had a very small heart, it could hold a rather large amount of gratitude." - A. A. Milne, *Winnie the Pooh*

Is there a connection between peak performance and gratitude? Can simply being thankful make you better at something? Is it worth exploring this as we try to develop better practice habits?

Even Winnie's pal Piglet recognized the value in having a large amount of gratitude in your heart. And he was right. Studies have shown the effects of gratitude or thankfulness can have a very positive impact on many areas of your life. Having the old *attitude of gratitude* seems to not be just a snazzy slogan uttered by the mass of motivational speakers, but looks like it is actually sound advice.

Psychologist Robert Emmons has been studying gratitude for years. His research shows that people who practice gratitude consistently have: stronger immune systems, lower blood pressure, sleep better, are more alert, have less stress, have more joy, are more outgoing and feel less lonely, along with a host of other benefits.

Gratitude can cause dopamine to be released in the brain

which as we have discussed, is a powerful tool that can help motivate us and drive us to rewards. Studies from the National Institutes of Health have shown that people with more gratitude have higher levels of activity in the hypothalamus. This area of the brain is responsible for regulating many things, along with releasing various hormones that contribute to everything from your sleep, to your overall mood, to your sex drive.

So the bottom line once we accept that gratitude is indeed creating some changes in our brains, is can we possibly harness this and can it affect our practice and performance.

Many of the aforementioned effects such as better sleep, or being more calm could certainly benefit us during performance time, or even at practice.

What is the best way to develop that attitude of gratitude? One of the best ways to pump up your thankful muscle is by keeping a *Gratitude Journal*. Many studies on gratitude include some sort of journaling or writing down things the participants are thankful for. You can do this with a journal that you write in daily or weekly. You can also get in the habit of pausing briefly throughout your day to think of something you are thankful for.

More specific to our practice time, taking a minute to think about being grateful for the opportunity to practice your skill is a great way to get yourself in the right mindset. It also helps to look at how much improvement you have had, and be thankful for the advancement you have seen.

I use a little gratitude exercise when I compete in Frisbee events with my dogs. There can be a lot of stress during events you are competing at when there are world titles or qualifying spots on the line. Keeping your stress in check is not only key to help you perform your best, but in the case of your canine partner, the last thing you want to do is have your stress affect them. Dog's are so sensitive that they can feel if you are loaded up with anxiety and it will likely show up in their performance.

Each time I step on the field I take a few seconds, look directly in my dog's eyes and say, "I am so thankful I get to play with you today." Then I just think about that for a couple more seconds. Not only does this affirm the fact that I really do appreciate this time with them, but it helps ease my nerves and takes the focus off the stress of competing. It makes me feel like I have already won!

The concept of saying what you are grateful for, or writing it down in a journal, is a great first step. However, the crucial part, and the part that often gets overlooked, is actually taking a little time to think about it. I have heard some say that they tried writing down what they were thankful for but it didn't seem to help them. That is kind of like just writing a goal down and then taking no action and not following through. It probably won't help. So when you are practicing gratitude, make sure you think about it, let it wash over you. Really *feel* that thankfulness. I think that is when you will start to see the benefit!

So try a little gratitude as part of your skill development, you might find that it is just what you need!

45: Conclusion

"The only true measure of success is the ratio between what we might have done and what we might have been on the one hand, and the thing we have made and the things we have made of ourselves on the other."
H.G. Wells

This is why I feel so passionate about the concept of getting better, and more specifically helping people practice more effectively and efficiently. I truly believe we can narrow that gap between what we might have done, and what we actually have done by getting organized with how we approach improving ourselves.

We all have so many things we want to get better at, and have the ability to do so, we just need a blueprint to follow to help get us there.

Throughout this book I have shared various concepts that will hopefully help you develop a clear picture of what's possible with practice. We have looked at various tips and techniques that can make practice pay off and keep us interested. Of course the SMART Practice Core System is the real catalyst for change. Implementing the principles of the SMART Practice Core System will help you improve any skill.

One of the things I see as I talk to groups about improving skills, is a lack of belief that real improvement can happen. I think this stems from a couple of things. First, there is often a history of trying to get better at something or "get it together," that hasn't worked out, and that's led to disappointment and ultimately an attitude of "why bother." Second, with so much of the focus of self improvement literature and coaching on *being the best in the world*, instead of just *being better tomorrow than you are today*, it can make improving seem like a daunting task.

The absolute best thing you can do for yourself if you want to get better at something, is to believe that regardless of what experience you have had in the past you can and will improve if you get organized with how you approach it and follow through.

Using the SMART Practice system will fix both the aforementioned issues. The reason you likely failed improving in the past was a lack of a clear plan to follow, so working with the system and tools in this book will give you the clarity you need. If you want to improve something, it is all about taking small steps, and they need to be the right steps for you! The focus here is on determining where you want to go, where you currently are, and then looking at the steps you need to take to get yourself to the next level. The cool thing about the SMART Practice system is it is customizable for exactly what you need to improve the skill you are working on. It isn't just some path that someone else took. It allows you to fine tune what you need.

If you have read through this book and haven't actually started working on improving a skill yet, then you are primed and ready to put this information into action.

It's up to you. You now have the tools and a step by step method for getting better. Decide in this moment to improve in some area, and then get started. Maybe it's getting better at something you are already good at and you want to take it to the next level. Maybe it's something you have struggled with and now you are committed to seeing some progress. Perhaps it is a new skill that you are going to finally commit to tackling. I'm sure you have something that you want to improve at some level... *now is your time!*

Henry David Thoreau beautifully encapsulated everything I believe about our ability to get better with this quote: "I know of no more encouraging fact than the unquestionable ability of man to elevate his life by conscious endeavor."

I am convinced beyond a shadow of a doubt, if you have something in your life that you would like to improve, and you apply the SMART Practice system, you will get positive results! If you practice the right things, in the right way, and put in the time - you WILL get better!

Notes

1: What Practice Is and Isn't

[1] The Role of Deliberate Practice in the Acquisition of Expert Performance
K. Anders Ericsson, Ralf Th. Krampe, and Clemens Tesch-Romer
Psychological Review 1993, Vol. 100. No. 3, 363-406

3: The Surge

[1] Malcolm Gladwell
Outliers: The Story of Success
Little, Brown and Company, November 18, 2008

4: Lucky or Good?

[1] Ringo Starr, Interviewed by Robyn Flans
Modern Drummer Magazine, Dec/Jan 1982
[2] David Epstein
The sports Gene: Inside the Science of Extraordinary Athletic Performance
Current, April 29, 2014

5: 10,000 Hours

[1] K. Anders Ericsson
The Danger of Delegating Education to Journalists: Why the APS Observer Needs Peer Review When Summarizing New Scientific Developments

Tallahassee, Florida, October 28th, 2012

6: The Merge

[1] Charles J. Limb
Emotional Intent Modulates The Neural Substrates Of Creativity: An fMRI Study of Emotionally Targeted Improvisation in Jazz Musicians
Scientific Reports 6, Article number: 18460 (2016)

[2] John Geirland, "Go With The Flow". Wired magazine, September, 1996 Issue 4.09

[3] Steven Kotler
The Rise of Superman: Decoding the Science of Ultimate Human Performance
New Harvest, March 4, 2014

7: Mindset

[1] Carol Dweck
Carol Dweck Revisits the 'Growth Mindset'
Education Week blog
September 22, 2014

[2] Carol Dweck
Mindset: The New Psychology of Success
Ballantine Books; Reprint, Updated edition, December 26, 2007

[3] Edward De Bono
The Use of Lateral Thinking
Intl Center for Creative Thinking, 1971

8: Blocked or Random

[1] Richard Schmidt and Tim Lee
Motor Control and Learning: A Behavioral
Human Kinetics Publishers; 3rd edition, 2005

10: Novelty and Surprise

[1] Emrah Duzel

Absolute Coding of Stimulus Novelty in the Human Substantia Nigra/VTA

Neuron, 2006

21: The Practice Minefield

[1] Steven Pressfield

The War of Art

Black Irish Entertainment LLC; January 11, 2012

22: Distractions

[1] Gloria Mark, Interview by Kermit Pattison

Worker, Interrupted: The Cost of Task Switching

Fast Company, 2008

[2] Clifford Nass

Study published in Proceedings of the National Academy of Sciences, 2009

24: Procrastination

[1] Steven Pressfield

The War of Art

Black Irish Entertainment LLC; January 11, 2012

28: Make it Easy

[1] Alison Jing Xu, Aparna A. Labroo

Incandescent affect: Turning on the hot emotional system with bright light

Journal of Consumer Psychology, 2014

[2] Holland RL, Sayers JA, Keatinge WR, Davis HM, Peswani R.

Effects of body temperature on reasoning, memory and mood
PubMed, 1986

32: 1%
[1] Pat Riley interview by LB GSCHWANDTNER
The Pat Riley Formula for a Winning Team
Selling Power Magazine
[2] Dave Brailsford interview by Matt Slater
BBC Sport, Aug 8, 2012

33: Right, Wrong, Right
[1] Daniel Coyle
The Talent Code
Bantam; 1 edition April 28, 2009

36: The Edge
[1] Daniel Coyle
The Talent Code
Bantam; 1 edition April 28, 2009

42: Perspective
[1] Sian Beilock
Choke or thrive? The relation between salivary cortisol and math performance depends on individual differences in working memory and math-anxiety. PubMed, 2011

Acknowledgements

I have had the pleasure of working with many enthusiastic students over the years on a variety of skills. Each time I have felt like I have learned as much from them as they have from me. Seeing someone have a breakthrough on something they have been working hard on never gets old.

The SMART Practice system was tested for years on thousands of willing students who provided amazing feedback and encouragement. Without their help it would have been much more difficult to determine what methods actually worked. I remain forever in their debt.

I need to thank the many teachers and mentors I have had over the years who have instilled principles of excellence in me. The encouragement of friends and peers along the path of trying to become a better coach and instructor has been invaluable.

My wife has inspired and encouraged me on the journey of writing this book. She served as my editor and helped keep my focus on what needed to be said. She is my rock. She IS the run-on-sentence police!

I want to thank God for giving me the desire to always reach beyond where I am, and for giving me the belief that with Him, anything is possible.

About the Author

As a professional musician, Jeff has released 9 albums, toured the world, and been featured in magazines in the U.S., Europe and Japan. He has written music for commercials for Toyota, Chevrolet and many others. He has done music for the *Style Network, Outdoor Channel, ESPN* and daytime TV shows like *All my Children*. He's shared the stage with ZZ Top, Cheap Trick, Poison, Cinderella, Joan Jett, .38 Special, ELO, Scorpions, and many more.

As a guitar educator he has released 9 video courses, and 1 book. As Director of Education for TrueFire he has worked with multiple Grammy-winning artists, crafting their curriculum and producing their video courses.

As a speaker he has performed at over 300 speaking engagements. He has written articles on practicing and skill aquisition for a wide variety of magazines.

He is trained daily by three extremely talented Frisbee dogs. Jeff and the dogs have performed at sold out arenas, been featured on *ESPN SportsCenter*, the cover of *Dogsport magazine*, and won multiple state and world championships.

Contact Jeff directly at: jeff@jeffscheetz.com